BEYOND ORIGINAL SIN

More Orbis Books by Diarmuid O'Murchu

Adult Faith

Ancestral Grace

Consecrated Religious Life

Evolutionary Faith

God in the Midst of Change

In the Beginning Was the Spirit

Incarnation: A New Evolutionary Threshold

Inclusivity: A Gospel Mandate

The Meaning and Practice of Faith

Religious Life in the Twenty-First Century

Transformation of Desire

BEYOND ORIGINAL SIN

❧

Recovering Humanity's Creative Urge

Diarmuid O'Murchu, MSC

ORBIS ✦ BOOKS
www.orbisbooks.com

Founded in 1970, Orbis Books endeavors to publish works that enlighten the mind, nourish the spirit, and challenge the conscience. The publishing arm of the Maryknoll Fathers and Brothers, Orbis seeks to explore the global dimensions of the Christian faith and mission, to invite dialogue with diverse cultures and religious traditions, and to serve the cause of reconciliation and peace. The books published reflect the views of their authors and do not represent the official position of the Maryknoll Society. To learn more about Maryknoll and Orbis Books, please visit our website at http://www.maryknollsociety.org.

Library of Congress Cataloging-in-Publication Data

Names: O'Murchu, Diarmuid, author.
Title: Beyond original sin : recovering humanity's creative urge / Diarmuid O'Murchu.
Description: Maryknoll : Orbis Books, 2018. | Includes bibliographical references and index.
Identifiers: LCCN 2018004578 (print) | LCCN 2018007942 (ebook) | ISBN 9781608337521 (e-book) | ISBN 9781626982864 (pbk.)
Subjects: LCSH: Sin, Original. | Fall of man.
Classification: LCC BT720 (ebook) | LCC BT720 .O25 2018 (print) | DDC 233—dc23
LC record available at https://lccn.loc.gov/2018004578

Contents

Introduction

Humans are on Earth like beings stricken with amnesia.

—Plato

By the end of the twenty-first century, religion is likely to undergo an unrelenting metamorphosis. With the increasingly rapid advances in information technology, more and more people will begin to question just about everything, and popular religiosity will not survive that onslaught. Correspondingly, the expanding gap between rich and poor, and the several fears around personal survival, will beget even more devotional practices, and many of these will be fueled by religious fundamentalism. Unfortunately, neither side of the polarized divide is likely to receive the kind of attention that would evoke rigorous research on the one hand, or informed spiritual discernment on the other. So, the malaise, the drifting, and the disturbing, violent fundamentalist outbursts are likely to continue unabated.

The present book may be described as a strategic intervention to bring about a modicum of change in the confused landscape. It is likely to exert the greatest appeal for adult faith seekers disillusioned with inherited religious wisdom and seeking an alternative that is far from clear. My desire is to build a bridge toward that alternative by a substantial rethinking of one of religion's most enduring postulates, namely, humanity's inherited spiritual depravity (usually referred to as *original sin*), in the face of which we need the intervention of a rescuing divine figurehead. Contrary to the long-held conviction that humans enter the world in a flawed sinful state, I propose, and seek to defend, the view that we enter the world as graced creatures, fundamentally good, and not essentially perverted.

I defend this view largely through the growing body of evidence arising from anthropology and paleontology (the study of human origins), material rarely accessed by either the social or religious sciences of our time. Furthermore, I argue that instead of bemoaning our inherited flaw—and forever awaiting a divine rescue—we need to embrace our foundational creativity and engage our world in a proactive way to support evolution's progressive unfolding. To rephrase the oft-quoted statement of Scripture scholar John Dominic Crossan (2010), instead of waiting on God's intervention, we need to wake up and respond to God's call for our collaboration.

To some it will sound as if I am trying to get rid of God, and I may end up being accused of creating a new anthropocentric Deity. I address this concern by revisiting the spiritual embeddedness of several indigenous peoples around the world, namely their faith in the Great Spirit, the oldest faith system known to humanity, one I have described in detail elsewhere (O'Murchu 2012). My aim is to redefine religion, not get rid of it. However, my strategy is highly original, entailing a radical revaluation of what religious faith is all about.

I come to this undertaking as a social scientist with a long interest in the evolutionary unfolding of religious sentiment and spiritual aspiration. Religionists do not like social scientists; we are often viewed as the ones who set out to wreck religious faith. We do not wreck it. We seek to illuminate its dysfunctional elements, particularly the childish dependencies that often ensue, and reconstruct a more mature, adult mode of spiritual engagement. In a word, we deconstruct in order to ⤶ reconstruct.

As a Christian, I want to wager my bets on that enduring sense of hope at the heart of my inherited faith. For me it is not the person of Christ understood according to ecclesiastical criteria, nor is it the friendly, innocuous Jesus of so much popular spirituality that matters. It is the prophetic, spirit-inspired figure who declared to the world a "new reign of God"—a daring, empowering, liberating vision, grounded not in Aristotelian anthropology (and its several derivatives from early church councils), nor the several imperial caricatures that ensued, but on the reclamation of a relational anthropology, long known to our ancient ancestors, and poised for a subversive comeback amid the breakdown and disintegration that characterizes our world today.

Humans are creatures with an ancient, complex story, one that rational knowledge has not handled well. And we are also evolutionary beings forever evoking wisdom from the future. The rich reservoirs of our past and the mystical openness to the ever new horizon are the broad strokes that guide and inspire the present work. Welcome to the exploration!

As It Was in the Beginning

The Old Testament never refers to the event of Genesis 3 as "the fall" and does not talk about people or the world as "fallen."

—John H. Walton

Humans, it seems, have been intrigued by origins from time immemorial. How did it all begin? And who or what caused the initial upsurge? While today we rely on science to answer such questions, up until the mid-twentieth century, people relied on other sources, many of which were religious in nature. How we integrate scientific wisdom with prescientific ideas is a central feature of the present work.

First, however, let's look at the ancient fascination around origins, as we seek to discern its speculative elements while also seeking to honor some deep, enduring truths. All myths of origin rely heavily on creative imagination and the human search for meaning, which is foundationally a spiritual pursuit. In some cases we can point to actual historical features. For instance, the various kings described in the Epic of Gilgamesh (written c. 2100 BCE) were significant figures in the Sumerian/Babylonian cultures of the time. What makes such myths both fascinating and enduring is their ability to awaken in peoples of different times and cultures foundational values that give meaning and direction to our lives.

Ancient Mythology

Research into myths of origin took a quantum leap in the twentieth century with the publication of Mircea Eliade's classic work (1961) *The Sacred and the Profane*. According to Eliade, myth narrates a sacred history, an event that took place in primordial time, the fabled time of the "beginnings." In other words, myth offers an imaginative construct of how the Divine operates, bringing reality into existence, be it in the whole of its cosmic grandeur or in the particularity of our planetary existence and our own human journey through life. In several such myths, creation arose *ex nihilo*—that is, "from nothing." But in many creation myths the line is blurred whether the creative act would be better classified as a creation *ex nihilo* or creation from chaos—a very important insight for a fuller understanding of the opening chapter of the book of Genesis.[1]

A number of recurring themes have been noted in myths of origin:

- The primeval abyss, an infinite expanse of waters or space.
- An originator Deity that is awakened or an eternal entity within the abyss.
- The originator Deity poised above the abyss.
- A cosmic egg or embryo.

---

[1] In African cosmologies especially, the earth is preexistent. A creation out of nothing occurs as a theme much less frequently than in our cultural contexts.

- The originator Deity creating life through sound or word.
- Life generating from the corpse or dismembered parts of an originator Deity.

Many of these themes occur in the book of Genesis and are explored later in this work. (More appears in Eliade 1961; 1963; Segal 2004.)

In our contemporary culture of scientific objectivity, rigorous analysis, and instrumental reasoning we are quick to dismiss anything to do with mythic origins. But as science itself becomes more interdisciplinary, we realize that ancient mythology carries an alternative kind of wisdom based on imagination, intuition, and creative insight, which we dismiss at our own peril. Without something of the subliminal wisdom of this ancient resource, we can all too quickly succumb to a robotlike existence that robs us of mystery and meaning. At the other end of the spectrum is the religious tendency to literalize myths of origin, a shortsighted pitfall for several foundational religions. David Christian alerts us to this danger when he writes,

> How did everything begin? This is the first question faced by any creation myth and . . . answering it remains tricky. . . . Each beginning seems to presuppose an earlier beginning. . . . Instead of meeting a single starting point, we encounter an infinity of them, each of which poses the same problem. . . . There are no entirely satisfactory solutions to this dilemma. What we have to find is not a solution but some way of dealing with the mystery. . . . And we have to do so using words. The words we reach for, from God to gravity, are inadequate to the task. So we have to use language poetically or symbolically; and such language, whether

used by a scientist, a poet, or a shaman, can easily be misunderstood. (2004, 17–18)

The dating of these myths of origin seems to me critically important, although almost impossible to establish with any degree of accuracy. The Judeo-Christian origin story (recorded in the book of Genesis) relies heavily on Sumerian-Babylonian legends while also incorporating material from Persian, Egyptian, and Greek sources. The Sumerians, composing the stories possibly as early as 3000 BCE, dated the origins of the world around 240,000 years ago. The Babylonians left it more open, suggesting that it could be anytime between 400,000 and 200,000 BCE.

The Egyptians, developing similar myths around the same time, claim that the reign of the Gods first occurred about 36,500 years ago. The Greeks (followed by the Romans) adopted a much more rational approach, maintaining that there is no way of asserting when the world began, and instead focused attention on the evolution of human culture from about 2500 BCE onward. Zoroastrianism involves a 12,000-year cosmology, drawn on an earlier evaluation from the older Persian culture. Since the birth of Zoroaster is a highly disputed issue— with dates varying from 1750 to 500 BCE—it is difficult to envisage when precisely their myths of origin were formulated.

Finally, in a Daoist creation myth, "The Way gave birth to unity; unity gave birth to duality; duality gave birth to trinity; trinity gave birth to the myriad creatures' (*Daodejing*, fourth century BCE). We note here that humans come on the scene after several other life forms have evolved and flourished. Several Chinese myths of origin follow a similar emphasis on relational process around the notion of the one and the many. The Indian *Rig Veda* echoes a similar evolutionary tone, inviting the devotee not to become too anthropocentric, rational, or speculative in engaging such questions:

Neither being (*sat*) nor non-being was as yet. What
was concealed? And where? And in whose protection?
. . . Who really knows? Who can declare it? Whence
was it born, and whence came this creation? The *devas*
were born later than this world's creation, so who
knows from where it came into existence? None can
know from where creation has arisen, and whether he
has or has not produced it. He who surveys it in the
highest heavens, he alone knows—or perhaps does not
know. (Rig Veda 10.129)

Some modern scientists, such as the late Carl Sagan and the
physicist Fritjof Capra, hold the view that the ancient religious
wisdom of the Far East is much more in tune with contemporary science than our Western Judeo-Christian inheritance.

Anthropocentric Myths of Power

I briefly outline these suggested datings in order to provide
context for the later reflections of this book. I ask the reader
to note that virtually all these myths were created within a
time span of five thousand years before the Christian era; in
fact, several of them belong to the period 2000–1000 BCE. In
cultural terms, this is the postagricultural era, within which I
locate what I later describe as the *shadow side* of the Agricultural Revolution. Central features of this emerging reality are
manifest in the following significant developments:

- Patriarchal domination
- Superiority of the rational mind
- Hierarchical ordering, with the kinglike God at the top
  of the pyramid
- Evolution of royal kingship
- Fragmentation and commodification of land

- Distrust and subversion of the feminine—possibly an anti-Goddess development
- Alienation between humans and the land/earth
- Increased levels of adversarial conflict
- Competitive violence leading in time to warfare[2]

The myths of origin are employed to explain the beginnings of the world and all that unfolds thereafter. It is remarkable how quickly they descend into human-animal conflict, or human-human competitive aggression. In the book of Genesis, chapter 1 describes the elegance and beauty of creation; the remaining forty-nine chapters are largely about the human craving for power and the violent strategies adopted to achieve it. Commentators are quick to conclude that it is wayward humans who disturb and destroy the divinely instituted equilibrium, but the reality is much more complex. As Karen Armstrong perceptively points out, God is creating the violent mess every bit as much as humanity:

> The God who dominates the first chapter of the Bible has disappeared from the human scene by the end of Genesis. Story after story reveals a much more disturbing God: as we shall see the omnipotent God of the first chapter soon loses control of his creation; the immutable Deity is seen to change his mind and even to feel threatened by humanity. The benevolent Creator becomes a fearful Destroyer. The impartial God who saw all his creatures as "good" now has favorites and teaches his proteges to behave in an equally unfair

---

[2] I am not denying the benefits that accrued from the Agricultural Revolution, which are widely assumed to be positive and constructive. In truth, very few commentators take such a positive view. See the informed analysis of Barker (2009); Manning (2004); Taylor (2005).

manner to their dependents. By the time we have reached the end of the text, almost every one of the expectations we were encouraged to form in Chapter 1 have been knocked down. (1996, 13)

When dealing with myths of origin we need to maintain a balance between the rational (literal) and the archetypal (imagination). The latter is what requires a great deal of discernment. The notion of archetypes (derived from two Greek words: *arche*, meaning first, and *tupos*, meaning type or form) tends to be associated with the psychologist Carl Jung to describe foundational values that primordially seem to belong to the living universe itself; subsequently they manifest in humans as sublime energetic forces, forever luring us into a deeper search for meaning.

The theologian Paul F. Knitter describes archetypes as

predispositions towards the formation of images, a-priori powers of representation, inbuilt stirrings or lures that, if we can feel and follow them, will lead us into the depths of what we are and where we are going. They might be called messages-in-code, which we must decode and bring to our conscious awareness. It is difficult to speak about what these messages contain. Their general contents, Jung tells us, have to do with light and darkness, death and rebirth, wholeness, sacrifice, and redemption. He saw such archetypes as the common seedbed of all religions. (1985, 57)

All myths of origin are primarily about the archetypal and not the rational. They are stories of creative imagination, compiled to help people comprehend the mystery within which we live and move and have our being. They represent the transcendent rather than the immanent. They transcend rationality and scientific verification, and need not be viewed as being in conflict with either. As a social scientist, it seems to me that one important function of science and rational wisdom is to illuminate archetypal content by aligning its various features with our everyday experience. Among other things this involves differentiating superficiality from depth, and highlighting enduring truth above and beyond the contextual conditioning of a particular culture, religion, or historical epoch.

The Genesis Narrative

Volumes have been written on myths of origin, and while the research indicates a range of possible interpretations, there is a substantial degree of consensus on the resume I provide at the beginning of this book. With such background we can now review the story of Genesis as the prevailing Judeo-Christian myth of origin.

The book of Genesis chronicles the creation of the world and everything in it, as well as God's early relationship with humans. It falls into two broad categories: (1) primeval history (chapters 1–11), which includes the story of creation, as well as that of Adam and Eve, Cain and Abel, and Noah; and (2) the patriarchal history (chapters 12–50), which includes the narratives of Abraham, Isaac, Jacob, and Joseph. Altogether, the stories in Genesis span—according to the usual calculation—2,369 years. The sources from which Genesis was compiled include Babylonian, Egyptian, and Hebrew myths and folklore, dating from the tenth to the fifth centuries BCE.

What modern peoples view as a uniform text actually comprises the work of three main authors known as the Yahwist (J), the Elohist (E), and the Priestly (P), with a composition time span ranging from about 950 BCE to 450 BCE. Genesis focuses primarily upon five persons: Adam, Noah, Abraham, Isaac, and Jacob (all males). God (also assumed to be male) appears repeatedly throughout the text, interacting with humans largely through issuing commands and announcements, and punishing, forgiving, or testing those who have been created.

For Christians generally, Genesis is about the downfall of humanity, with the woman, Eve, being the primary culprit. Christians seem to easily forget that the narrative begins with the repeated declaration that all in creation is good. However, the storyline quickly moves from divine benevolence to human precariousness. Adam and Eve collude in betraying an original idyllic wholeness, and thereafter disaster and violence explode throughout the entire plot.

Why was the book of Genesis written? Many scholars suggest that Genesis should be viewed within the Pentateuch—Genesis, Exodus, Leviticus, Numbers, and Deuteronomy—with entry to the promised land as its ultimate goal. Genesis begins with God's people dwelling safely in Eden, disrupted through sin and exile, and ends with God's people dwelling in safety in Egypt. More specifically, it records the covenant that God made with the people of Israel, the establishment of which was entrusted primarily to Abraham and his descendants.

Archetypally, Genesis depicts a God who forever remains faithful, a God who keeps promises and provides refuge for the wandering people. No matter what sin happens to the people, around them, or even from them, they know deep within that they are the beneficiaries of an enduring loyalty—hence, the covenantal basis of the Hebrew faith. Wes Howard-Brook (2010; 2016) is a leading voice among contemporary scholars who maintains that it is the elegant creation itself (Chapter 1 of Genesis) that forms the core element of covenantal allegiance. I return to his insights later.

Overtly, however, the outcome is quite different. At its face value much of the Genesis story is about human rebellion, sin, betrayal, and disappointment. God's fidelity also takes some strange twists and turns, with divinely sanctioned violence reaching disturbing proportions. These deviations may belong more to later commentators, and many would regard St. Augustine as the one who departed most significantly from the original foundational wisdom in the Hebrew Scriptures.

St. Augustine's Contribution *to O. Sin*

Augustine of Hippo (354–430) is widely regarded as the one who popularized the notion of *original sin*, providing the doctrinal basis upon which it became an indisputable article of Christian faith. The Augustinian theory affirms that, by virtue of organic unity, the whole human race existed in Adam at the time of his transgression. It claims that Adam's will was the will of the species, so that in Adam's act of rebellion, the whole race revolted against God, thus incurring a subsequent state of corruption. In Adam, all humans existed as one moral person, and with Adam's downfall we brought upon ourselves a permanent condemnation to sin and lawlessness.

Augustine did not actually devise the concept of original sin, but his use of specific New Testament Scriptures to justify the doctrine was new. The concept itself had been shaped from the late second century onward by certain church fathers, including Irenaeus, Origen, and Tertullian. Irenaeus did not use the Scriptures at all for his definition, Origen reinterpreted the Genesis account of Adam and Eve in terms of a Platonic allegory and saw sin deriving solely from free will, and Tertullian's version was borrowed from Stoic philosophy.

Though Augustine was convinced by the arguments of his earlier patristic peers, he made use of Paul's letters, especially Romans, to develop his own ideas on original sin and guilt. The key text is that of Romans 5:12–21:

Romans 5:12

Therefore, just as sin came into the world through one man, and death came through sin, and so death spread to all because all have sinned. . . . If, because of the one man's trespass, death exercised dominion through that one, much more surely will those who receive the abundance of grace and the free gift of righteousness exercise dominion in life through the one man, Jesus Christ. Therefore just as one man's trespass led to condemnation for all, so one man's act of righteousness leads to justification and life for all. For just as by the one man's disobedience the many were made sinners, so by the one man's obedience the many will be made righteous.[3] *Who influenced whom? Augustine, Irenaeus, Origin, Tertullian*

Following the Latin commentary of the anonymous Ambrosiaster (whom Augustine names as Hilary), Augustine misread the original Greek. Instead of reading the text as "because all have sinned," Augustine read it, "in whom all have sinned," thus creating the notion of sinning in Adam, thus inheriting Adam's *guilt* as well as his *corruption. For Augustine, such depravity was transmitted through biological inheritance, specifically through sexual propagation.* Historically, this interpretation of sinning in Adam did not exist prior to the end of the fourth century.

For this reason, Augustine made the claim that all humanity sinned "in Adam." All humans came into being from Adam's semen, or as later theologians contended, because Adam was the "federal head" of humanity. Later in the same chapter of Romans, Paul juxtaposes the sin of Adam with the righteous-

---

[3] The *Catechism of the Catholic Church* follows a very similar line of argument, explaining that in "yielding to the tempter, Adam and Eve committed a *personal sin*, but this sin affected *the human nature* that they would then transmit in a *fallen state*. . . . [O]riginal sin is called 'sin' only in an analogical sense: it is a sin 'contracted' and not 'committed'—a state and not an act" (*Catechism of the Catholic Church*, 404).

ness of Christ. So Augustine's key argument is based on a translation error, a chief reason why so many contemporaries regard the theory of original sin as theologically untenable.

Three features of this inherited understanding are particularly problematic for the anthropological approach I am using throughout this book:

- *Exalting the biological dimension of human nature above and beyond other aspects.* Augustine may have inherited this approach from Aristotle, whose understanding of the human we explore later.
- *The demonization of human sexuality*, which has caused serious ethical, psychological, and spiritual problems down through the ages.
- *The demonization of death itself* (also supported, it seems, by St. Paul). Death did not come into the world through Adam, nor is death an evil to expel. Death is an integral, God-given dimension of all life forms, cosmic and creaturely alike.

Why did Augustine become so preoccupied with such matters, leaving us with such a seriously distorted view of humanity? Judging from his *Confessions,* Augustine himself seems to have had an emotionally turbulent upbringing, particularly with the loss of his father at age seventeen and the later influence of an overly protective and moralistic mother (Monica). As a teenager he seems to have indulged in a sexually fluid lifestyle, followed by a nonmarital but stable fifteen-year relationship, out of which his son, Adeodatus, was born. He had hoped to enter a subsequent relationship but made a rather sudden switch to a celibate life, a shift so abrupt it is widely interpreted as being heroic, but one wonders about the repressive forces that may have been at work in his life, impacting, among other things, his theory of original sin.

Instead of focusing on Augustine's personal story, several scholars highlight other influences, particularly of a philosophical nature. He first became a disciple of the Manicheans, a Gnostic-Christian sect that taught, among other things, that all matter is inherently evil. They also denied the real incarnation of Christ, as well as his bodily resurrection, because of their view of the essentially evil nature of matter, including the human body. Augustine's nine years with them may have deeply influenced his anthropology especially in relation to human embodiment and sexuality.

Augustine's legacy in regard to original sin, while historically significant for the theologian, is highly problematic for the anthropologist. It leaves us with a distorted, imbalanced view of human nature, overly reliant on culturally restricted philosophical views and a misinformed use of Scripture. Augustinian scholars would want me to acknowledge his altruistic side: despite the perversity of the human condition, Augustine had no doubt that the grace and love of God could reach and transform even the most notorious sinner. Throughout subsequent chapters of this book I allude to the power of such unconditional love.

Evolutionary Considerations

I want to complete this overview of original sin by alluding to one of the major counterarguments of our time, namely, that this theory—and its link to the book of Genesis—makes very little evolutionary sense. With the wisdom of sciences like evolution, paleontology and anthropology, Genesis leaves us with not merely a morally depraved image of our species but one no longer capable of sustaining credulity in the twenty-first century. This dilemma is addressed in the compendium of Cavanaugh and Smith (2017). A group of ten authors of various Christian persuasions set out to acknowledge that the current scientific consensus points to the evolution of humans from primates, not as an original pair but through a gradual process of complex growth and development. Moreover, the emergence of humans from primates leaves little room for an original historical state of innocence from which humanity suffered a "fall." Clearly humans err and are fallible, but that "sinful" condition cannot be traced to an original rebellion whereby a state of paradisiacal harmony was forever destroyed, and can only be rectified by divine intervention in an act of redemptive rescue.

Increasingly, theologians wish to adopt the insights of the evolutionary sciences, yet they also wish to retain allegiance to the inherited Christian tradition of a fundamental flaw (original sin). Such fidelity to tradition seems to be desirable on three fronts. First, despite the complex—and often metaphorical—nature of the book of Genesis, it encapsulates a historical core, as well as revealed wisdom, which should not be dismissed as mere myth. Second, the story of the fall in Genesis reveals an indisputable fact about our human condition, as a wayward, sinful species. Finally, without such a cultural narrative calling us to a deeper awareness of our waywardness and our consequent moral responsibilities, we are living with gross self-deception, highly destructive of all life forms, our own included.

Undoubtedly, our postmodern world requires the theologian to be versed in multidisciplinary wisdom and to integrate such learning into theological discernment. Science, on the other hand, needs to acknowledge that theology embraces a sense of ultimacy beyond the focus of instrumental reason. The ensuing tension cannot be resolved merely by Stephen J. Gould's nonoverlapping magisteria (NOMA), since neither modern science nor theology are hidebound anymore by the rationality of Greek metaphysics or the theological import of St. Augustine's flawed anthropology. Intuition, imagination, and creativity are now central features of all organic, evolutionary inquiry.

Context, therefore, becomes critical if we hope to reach toward more discerning depth. While all the contributors to the Cavanaugh and Smith compendium (2017) agree that a literal interpretation of Genesis is no longer tenable, they offer reflections of a linguistic and religious nature that steer very close to literalism. None of the authors even allude to the suggestion that Genesis may have been written against the background of the Agricultural Revolution (cf. Taylor 2005; Snodgrass 2011). Much of the conflict and violence throughout the book of Genesis strongly reflects the abandonment of the more egalitarian relationship to the land (as in the hunter-gatherer culture) that seems to have prevailed in preagricultural times.

Analysis of the *garden,* the *woman,* and the *snake* all require expansive review beyond the immediate literary or linguistic context. Symbolically, the garden seems to denote paradise, the archetypal abode of harmony and fruitfulness. The woman seems quite at home in the garden and seems to enjoy an organic connection with the tree of life. Here, we may need to recall that the tree is a very ancient religious symbol, frequently used to depict the Great Earth Mother Goddess.[4] In archetypal terms, might that be the woman we are encountering in the book of Genesis? If so, it changes everything!

Are we then evidencing the misogynist bias of the emerging patriarchal domination, seeking to demonize the female and her organic link with the earth, the soil, and the land for much of the preagricultural era? And when she takes the fruit from the tree of life, reminiscent of her own embodied fertility, are we not witnessing something of the prodigious fertility long associated with the Great Mother Goddess? (For more, see Reid-Bowen 2007; Christ and Plaskow 2016.) She wants

---

[4] See more at http://herbmuseum.ca/content/goddess-and-tree-life.

to share the fruit with the rational patriarchal male, but he no longer knows how to receive it! And instead of viewing the avaricious male as the one who is out of step, the woman is blamed for the ensuing mess.

In a similar context, are not many commentators missing the deeper truth of the snake—perhaps better called a serpent? In the ancient Goddess culture this is a symbol for creativity and the power of sexuality. The snake also denotes the process of transformation that leads to healing (hence the snake in the Asklepian symbol of medicine). Once again the story in Genesis demonizes the symbol in the patriarchal drive to disempower—maybe, destroy—the power of the feminine principle.

Little wonder that from that moment on (Genesis 3), violence erupts and becomes an integral dimension of all the monotheistic religions for the next several centuries. Indeed, that does mark a serious deviation—a fundamental flaw— in humanity's evolutionary story. But it does not belong to the original myth of creation; it is born out of the major agricultural dislocation of eight thousand to ten thousand years ago.

Before that time, humans were certainly not perfect. Such perfection makes no evolutionary sense. Neither is it congruent for a species born into a state of creative freedom. Evolution at every level—including the human—involves learning through time, a process often described as coevolution (Thompson 1994; Nuismer 2017). A growing body of anthropological and paleontological evidence shows that when humans remain very close to the natural world—to the earth, soil, and land—they tend to get it right (never perfect). When we become separated—and alienated—from the land (as happened in the Agricultural Revolution) then we can get things badly wrong, and that, I suggest, is a far more congruent and credible context for our understanding of original sin.

Moving On

In making this critique of original sin and its grounding in the book of Genesis, it is not my intention to dismiss a topic that may still be of relevance and significance for theologians and those committed to protecting the doctrinal truths of one or another religious denomination. I am addressing the issue from an anthropological and paleontological base, dimensions that heretofore have been largely ignored or neglected in the religious domain and now need to be reclaimed for a more empowering theological stance. Such additional wisdom will offer quite a different view of human nature and of our spiritual growth and development over millennia rather than within the limited context of the past few thousand years.

In the next chapter I introduce what anthropology has to bring to our understanding of the human condition, highlighting the distortions of recent millennia precisely because we chose either to ignore or bypass anthropological wisdom. Moving beyond such inherited distortions, I then devote chapter 3 to delineating the new anthropological foundations that will sustain the more integrated vision developed throughout the subsequent chapters of this book. The outcome poses major challenges not merely for theology and science but for all forms of knowledge that impinge upon our human nature and its future destiny.

We are not, and never have been, a perfect species, but our existence holds more than we have heretofore acknowledged—and the time has come to name and celebrate that new and empowering horizon.

2

Our Inherited Anthropology

While anthropology as a formal discipline owes its origins to colonialism, the questions that have motivated anthropologists extend far back into classical antiquity, if not before.

—Mark Moberg

The twentieth century has been described as the most violent in recorded human history, with the atrocities of two world wars as primary evidence. That same century also gave us the killing fields of Pol Pot in Cambodia, the Rwandan genocide, and the thousands of "disappeared" victims of military repression in several Latin American countries. Nor do we seem to be learning much from such barbarities, as evidenced in the savage violence of Iraq, Afghanistan, Syria, Yemen, Somalia, Sri Lanka, and Myanmar throughout the opening decades of the twenty-first century. There is much to suggest that things are not improving for *Homo sapiens*; to the contrary, we seem to be on a sliding slope into annihilation, with some arguing that we are destroying planet Earth itself with our reckless and violent behavior.

Faced with such a dismal prognosis, some try to rationalize our plight by referencing the initial human predicament at the beginning of our time on earth. For Christians, it is recorded in the book of Genesis, the first book of the Judeo-Christian Bible. This myth of origin is only one among many, but for a range of complex reasons, the Genesis narrative has assumed enormous cultural import, adopted and promoted by all three monotheistic religions (Judaism, Christianity, and Islam). The cultural popularity of this myth reaches far beyond the religions that uphold it. Colonial movements ever since Roman times, and with additional fervor from the sixteenth century onward, used the Genesis myth to subdue several other peoples and cultures. Others aver that the basic common sense embedded in the Genesis story—suggesting that humans are innately violent—is the single greatest factor supporting its popularity.

As indicated in chapter 1 of this volume, the exclusive focus on religious myths of origin lacks credibility for our interdisciplinary age, in which a multidisciplinary wisdom is essential for an in-depth analysis of any living reality. Moreover, such a diversely rich context is also essential for a more mature and empowering form of Christian discernment.[1] The

---

[1] Christian discernment describes the human effort to discover, appropriate, and integrate God's desires for our growth and development as people of faith. In its popular (Ignatian) sense it is very much an individual process between the person and God, with the spiritual director acting as a kind of facilitator. Group discernment is a more loosely defined process, often invoked in areas of pastoral accountability. In the ecclesiastical context, discernment is understood to be the divinely bestowed prerogative of the teaching authority of the church—to which all other forms of discernment need to be accountable. In a world and church becoming increasingly suspicious of the integrity and truth of institutional guidance, the task of discernment for the future will become much more localized, dialogically mediated, and informed by the skills and wisdom of systems theory. Increasingly, personal and group discernment will interweave, with wisdom from the ground up, commanding much stronger credibility than

expanded horizon draws heavily on the social sciences, particularly those of evolution, paleontology, and anthropology. I begin this enlarged exploration outlining the foundational wisdom of contemporary anthropology.

The Study of the Human

Anthropology denotes the study of human beings across time and culture—how they adapt to various environments, communicate, and socialize with one another. Anthropologists are concerned with many aspects of people's lives: the everyday practices as well as the more dramatic rituals, ceremonies, and processes that define us as human persons. Despite the fact that the human species is the focus of attention, anthropology is not a widely known field of study. It is popularly understood as being about bones and fossils, predominantly of tribal peoples living in the distant past in remote areas of the planet.

The first formal reference to anthropology as an academic discipline comes from the University of Copenhagen in 1647. It began to gain recognition in French universities throughout the nineteenth century. The first formal endorsement in the United States came with the establishment of the American Ethnological Society in 1842. The study of human evolution, and particularly the publication in 1859 of Charles Darwin's *On the Origin of Species*, became the catalyst for a range of anthropological studies throughout the late nineteenth and twentieth centuries.

Throughout the latter half of the twentieth century, all the social sciences have been undergoing a paradigm shift. The impact on anthropology is outlined by Moberg (2013), who notes a significant move from the colonial, imperial, Western

---

that which comes from the top down. And multidisciplinary insight will be important for more wholesome outcomes.

self-righteousness to a more multidisciplinary, critical analysis
of observable data relating to peoples and their various cultural
conditions. Transcending the us-vs.-them dualistic split so often
adopted in the past, anthropologists today seek more objective
outcomes, which in several cases indicate that cultural conditions and ensuing personal behaviors were often a great deal
more complex than we have hitherto recognized.

Up until the mid-1800s, anthropology, like several other
sciences, was considered a sub-branch of philosophy, and philosophy's understanding of the human person heavily influenced anthropological research well into the twentieth century.
Of particular significance was the body/mind distinction, often
explored through the body/soul polarity. The theories of classical Greek philosophers—Herodotus, Socrates, Plato, Aristotle—exerted an influence far more powerful than previously
understood.

Enter Greek Philosophy

Philosophy, described as "love of wisdom," came into existence
as Greek thinkers grew ever more dissatisfied with supernatural and mythical explanations of reality. Over time, the Greeks
began to suspect that the universe had a rational or logical
order. Aristotle, a student of Plato, introduced a new emphasis
with substantial implications for the study of anthropology,
claiming that the human person was uniquely endowed with
logos, the power for reasoning. Only the human person (by
which Aristotle meant the male gender) shares with his fellow
humans the common and universal values upon which society
is based.

For Aristotle, the most authoritative aspect of our humanity is rationality, the capacity through which one can make
willed, free choices, above and beyond any environmental
influences. (See his *Nicomachean Ethics* 10.4.1166a.14–17;

9.1166a.22–23). Humans therefore are free and autonomous beings who make choices and direct the power of will to achieve what they believe will bring happiness (*eudaimonia*). But sometimes the object of desire does not bring true happiness, functioning instead to stunt growth and development, ultimately enslaving humans themselves. In this sense, human beings bear responsibility for their freely willed choices and have no one else to blame.

According to Patrick Chabal (2012), rationality conveys a surface truth, which on closer examination not merely lacks depth but turns out to be a form of cultural conceit. Equating rationality with the objectivity of science—and the ensuing mechanistic view of all creation—instrumental reason bypasses a range of other perceptions based on people's lived experience. Rationality frequently involves dichotomous splitting (dualisms), which begets clarity but often at the cost of underrating the complexity of life, as in the ecological challenges facing humanity today (see Plumwood 2002).

Harald Thorsrud, among others, highlights what he considers to be Aristotle's conflicted anthropology:

> Aristotle is conflicted about the nature and function of human beings. In Book IX of his *Nicomachean Ethics*, he asserts that what is most human is our rationality under the guidance of the executive authority of the practical intellect, and in Book X that it is exclusively the theoretical intellect, and its teleological authority. And so in keeping with the functional argument, he is conflicted about human happiness. If we take his advice in Book IX and identify with our practical intellect, our happiness will be constituted by the exercise of a collection of rational activities. The cost of doing so is to demote contemplation, to a position commensurate with the exercise of practical rationality. And if

we follow the advice in Book X and identify with our theoretical intellect, our happiness will be constituted exclusively with one rational activity. (2015)

Volumes have been written on Aristotle's anthropology, which is generally recognized to be quite dense and complicated. I am highlighting one dimension—namely, *rationality*—which became a central feature of subsequent scholastic philosophy in the Middle Ages, particularly under the influence of St. Thomas Aquinas, who, in turn, guided several subsequent generations of Christian theologians. And for cultures influenced by Christianity—European nations, and the many lands colonized by Europeans—Aristotle's anthropology acquired a universal significance that prevails until the present time. The following are some of the subtle derivatives that underlie the human predicament I am seeking to address in the present work:

- The human person is separated from the natural world. Being an ensouled, rational creature, the human stands superior and opposed to all other life forms.
- Dualistic splitting infiltrates human anthropology, as in the binary opposites of soul vs. body, matter vs. spirit, reason vs. feeling.
- The emphasis on rationality begins to create a serious dislocation of intuition, imagination, and creativity.
- Masculinity becomes the norm for all authentic human behavior.
- In subtle and overt ways, Aristotelian thought was used to buttress colonial imperialism, even in our understanding of God as a ruling king.
- Particularly significant for the present work, everything before the age of rationality was dismissed as primitive, barbaric, prelogical, and not to be taken seriously.

The Fundamental Flaw

After Aristotle, Augustine of Hippo is probably the next greatest influence we need to note. As indicated in chapter 1, he is the main architect of the Christian notion of original sin. Augustine saw the human being as a perfect unity of two substances: soul and body. Augustine's favorite image to describe *body-soul* unity is that of marriage: *caro tua, coniux tua* (your body is your wife). According to Augustine, the two elements were initially in perfect harmony. After the fall of humanity they are now experiencing dramatic combat between one another.

For Augustine, soul is a kind of substance, participating in reason, fit for ruling the body. (For Aristotle, the power of reasoning is also passed on through male semen.) Although the human is a composite of body and soul, soul is superior to the body, a claim Augustine made in his hierarchical classification of things into those that merely exist, those that exist and live, and those that exist, live, and have intelligence or reason.

Many other philosophers theorize on the human condition, but most build on the foundational insights of Aristotle and Augustine. Thus, the human is envisaged as uniquely endowed with a superior quality of life—above and beyond all other creatures on earth—yet is bedeviled with a fundamental flaw because of which one never gets things right. The nearest the human can hope to get things right is through a faithful and persistent use of the *power of reason*, informed by a quality of divine guidance known as *grace*. Men stand some chance of attaining this breakthrough, but women just don't have what is required; in the notorious words of Aristotle, repeated by St. Thomas Aquinas, women are misbegotten males (a derogatory denunciation that no Christian church has ever formally abrogated).

The inherited fundamental flaw came to be known as the doctrine of original sin, not merely a lynchpin of Christian theology, but rather something akin to an ideology of substantial cultural import. This was based initially on a rather literalized interpretation of the book of Genesis. In the popular imagination, it has been effectively elaborated by such literary works as Milton's *Paradise Lost,* which has poisoned human consciousness even more severely than the formal theology (ideology). It goes like this:

> Everything in heaven was whole and harmonious until one powerful angel, called Lucifer, got strange ideas, feeling that he could both challenge and transcend the mighty power of God himself. And he persuaded other angels that this feat could be accomplished. They say pride was Lucifer's downfall, leading to the great sin of disobedience. Michael, another powerful archangel, got whiff of what was brewing and rallied an alternative force. Battle broke out between the two groups. Michael and his cohort proved to be victorious, kicking Lucifer (Satan or the dragon) out of heaven. The defeated angels landed on earth, condemned thereafter to a nonangelic status called human nature. They began propagating through sexual intercourse, thus spreading their evil contagion not merely across the emerging human population but right into every aspect of creation. And the conduit through which the contagion spread was sex, understood to be a fierce instinctual drive.

There you have it: a most powerful ideological myth![2]

---

[2] Throughout this book I use the notion of myth to denote a type of narrative that occurs transculturally in our human search for meaning, stories that cannot be dismissed as fictional tales or superstitious legends, but highly symbolic narratives into which we are drawn intellectually and emotionally, both consciously and unconsciously. When a myth is working, it creates an idealized picture seeking a worldview that is relatively coherent,

Throughout Christendom, it was frequently considered to be literally true. Today, it is still cherished by fundamentalist scholars who surface a range of texts (mainly from the books of Daniel in the Old Testament and from Revelation in the New Testament) to substantiate the myth. More progressive scholars do not take it literally, with many dismissing the theory of original sin as having no basis in the Christian Scriptures (cf. Spong 1998; Williams 2001; Wiley 2002; McFarland 2010).

In terms of the inherited anthropology, we need to note the following elements:

- The notion of an original utopian state in which all humans coexisted in harmonic innocence makes no sense in an evolutionary universe. It is a deluded belief, based on the notion of an omnipotent, perfect God as postulated by monotheism and Greek metaphysics, which in turn postulates an original perfect human alongside the all-powerful Deity.
- Lucifer's hunger for power marks a primordial irruption of the human urge for absolute control. This urge is not born from some ancient Satanic instinct but from humanity's own confused patriarchal projections. In other words, we seek out mythological, angelic figureheads to compensate for our inability to obtain the quality—and quantity—of earthly power that we desire.
- And how do humans try to obtain that power? By setting up a demonized, dualistic force with which we can engage in battle. The heavenly battle, therefore, is a mirror image of the earthly strategy of competi-

---

harmonious, sensible, and therefore meaningful, so that life seems worth living. Although somewhat dated, the short and comprehensive overview of the renowned anthropologist Claude Lévi-Strauss (d. 1992) is still valuable (Lévi-Strauss 1978). For the general reader, I recommend McIntosh (2004).

tive conflict adopted by patriarchal males in order to reclaim their power.

- Pride and disobedience become the primary sins that preoccupy the patriarchs. They continue to be major moral infringements for all patriarchal religions.
- Humans assume an inflated existence, what Steve Taylor (2005) calls *the ego explosion*. They become the superior species, seeking to control everything within and around them. Creation becomes a mere commodity for human usufruct, the mechanistic view of creation, so problematic for our own time.
- In terms of the growth and flourishing of the human, the dichotomy between power and powerlessness controls and pollutes the entire plot. Most people end up trapped in powerlessness and therefore can never hope to realize the fuller potential of their God-given humanity.

The Wider Religious Landscape

Thus far, I am suggesting that our conventional inherited anthropology—our way of understanding human nature—is highly problematic and far from wholesome. Both the cultural influence of the ancient Greeks and the moralistic perceptions of the Judeo-Christian religion leave us with several serious liabilities. The ensuing understanding of our humanity is deviant and dysfunctional, seriously undermining our evolutionary growth and development. The fact that we have operated out of this paradigm for some three thousand years must not excuse us from probing more deeply. We need to get rid of some substantial inherited baggage.

How then do we reclaim a more authentic understanding of the human project? Already we get vital clues by looking at those major cultural traditions immediately preceding us—

going back to about 5000 BCE. Jewish scholars claim that the term *original sin* is unknown to the Jewish Scriptures, and the church's teachings on this doctrine are antithetical to the core principles of the Torah and the Hebrew prophets. Yet even a cursory review of the Old Testament depicts a rather violent God[3] who likes to punish enemies for their transgressions, and God is frequently depicted as a distant overseer whose mercy and forgiveness can only be accessed by a select few (e.g., Moses) and can only be appeased by temple-based rituals of atonement.

The situation is similar in the older religions: for both Hinduism and Buddhism, humans are essentially good, yet karma never seems too far away, and it may take several life cycles before the soul is eventually liberated into the state of nirvana. Ancient Chinese religion probably arose from animistic beliefs and shamanistic practices, but most research highlights the emergence of the Confucian influences from the Shang dynasty (1760–1120 BCE) onward; here the emphasis is on the basic goodness of humans as long as they live virtuously and abide by the expectations of learning and education as set in place by the wise leaders.

The African religious landscape is more difficult to access and is frequently dismissed as animistic and primitive. However, many of those tribal religions carry a sophisticated belief in the notion of the Great Spirit, as a transpersonal life force rather than a personal Deity (more in chapter 4 below), whereby the

---

[3] Cf. Schwager (2000, 60): "The Hebrew Bible contains 1,000 verses where God's own violent actions of punishment are described, 100 passages where Yahweh expressly commands others to kill people, and several stories where God kills or tries to kill for no apparent reason. Violence is easily the most often mentioned activity and central theme of the Hebrew Bible." For a fine overview of how violence is invoked in different religions, see Rowley (2014). An extensive bibliography is available at https://en.wikipedia.org/wiki/Religious_violence.

role of humanity is generally seen as one of harmonizing nature with the supernatural. From this brief overview we can detect a religious/spiritual movement from the narrow anthropocentric focus to a transpersonal expanding horizon:

- For the monotheistic religions of Judaism, Christianity, and Islam, the wholeness of humanity is strongly invested in the rational principle, a primary endowment of the male gender, with God imaged primarily as a male, patriarchal, royal figurehead (despite the theological notion of God as Trinity and its accompanying relational emphasis, discernible in all the great religions).
- For Hinduism, the oldest of the great Eastern religions, the dualistic split between humanity and divinity has largely disappeared, with the human endowed with the inner potential to become more God-like and eventually achieving it in the liberation of nirvana. Buddhism adopts a similar anthropology but becomes somewhat stuck in the desire to escape from suffering.[4]
- The African religions go much deeper, congruent with Africa being humanity's oldest homestead. There is a strong relational undercurrent, inclusive of all other sentient beings in a convivial relationship with the living Earth itself. The aliveness of the Earth, and of every life form therein, belongs to the Great Spirit. Several commentators, versed in Western rationality, tend to dismiss this spirit-infused spirituality as animism; they grossly misinterpret the deeper meaning.

---

[4] A central goal of Buddhism is the end of human suffering, which is to be achieved by the cessation of all desire. How desire is understood in Buddhism is quite complex, with selfish or inordinate desire being the focus of attention, although frequently this is not stated explicitly. For a more positive and empowering view of desire, see O'Murchu (2007).

Entering Deep Time

Chronologically, as we move backward into deep time, we have arrived at the wake of the Agricultural Revolution some ten thousand years ago. This is a critical juncture in tracing the evolution of formal religion and the problematic view of human nature outlined above. Sadly, most researchers do not even it. Consider this overview from the Australian evolutionary thinker John Stewart:

> For most of the last 100,000 years up until about 10,000 years ago, humans lived as foragers in small multi-family cooperative bands of a few tens of people. These bands were typically linked into cooperative tribal societies of a few hundred to a few thousand people. The bands within a tribe met regularly and shared common beliefs and cultural backgrounds. . . . Inculcated moral codes and social norms that were passed from generation to generation controlled the behavior of the people within bands and within each tribe to produce cooperative organization. And the codes also organized members of the group to punish any individuals who broke the codes. Unlike the more complex hierarchical human societies that began to emerge about 10,000 years ago, powerful kings or rulers did not govern the earlier bands and tribes. External management played no role in the organization of cooperation. A distinctive feature of the codes and norms that organized these tribal societies is that they tended to produce egalitarian behavior. (2000, 233)

After the Agricultural Revolution, things changed dramatically, and not for the better. According to American environmental journalist Richard Manning (2004), hunter-gatherers ate a wider variety of tasty foods, worked far less, and lived much more sensually and convivially than "civilized" humans. About ten thousand years ago, a new agrarian acquisitiveness evolved as humans sequestered land to grow crops for commercial gain—the first wealth inequality known to our species (according to Manning). Patriarchal modes of governance came to the fore, adopting hierarchical structures and aggressive domination. Violent competition became normative, and as humans became alienated from the land, a vast range of formerly unknown infectious diseases began to spread extensively—including influenzas, smallpox, measles, and tuberculosis.

As a species we had lost our grounding in the natural world. Before farming and cities we were wild humans. Ever since then, more and more of us have been tamed, which is making us ill and alienated (see Manning 2014). And that which has long been presumed to have advanced our relationship with the land actually began to alienate us from it. Whereas our previous egalitarian behavior had matured into a range of rituals celebrating the nourishing and empowering presence of the Great Spirit (more in O'Murchu 2012), a new patriarchal religion of power, domination, and control now came to the fore. The British archaeologist Graeme Barker concludes his study of the Agricultural Revolution with these words:

> Theism usually appears to have involved new concepts of human destiny being in the laps of the Gods, of sexuality being a threatening force, and of land being something to be controlled and pacified, of an ancestor which only gave its wealth in return for favors rendered. The cosmologies that developed in tandem with the agrarian-based, Greco-Roman, Judeo-Christian-Muslim, and Eastern religions of our world asserted

the primacy of the human over the natural world, a
primacy that is proving increasingly dangerous to sustain. (2009, 414)

As already indicated, some contemporary theologians
claim that there is no scriptural basis for the doctrine of original sin. As a social scientist I find it a far more insightful and
compelling argument to trace its source to the shadow side of
the Agricultural Revolution. This is where things seem to have
gone drastically wrong for the human species, and the addictive
urge to dominate, commodify, and control was buttressed and
made respectable by the rise of the rational mind about three
thousand years ago.[5] Meanwhile a number of other developments reinforce the growing alienation of human beings: the
evolution of kingship (about six thousand years ago), the culture of adversarial violence (the philosophy of divide and conquer), and perhaps most serious of all, the invention of the
father-God, ruling from above the sky. The long-lived matristic,
organic understanding of the divine (the Goddess) had come
to a rather abrupt end, and humans began to suffer intense
anomie—from God, from nature, and from their true selves.

As we enter the Christian era, the culture of rationality
subverts the more egalitarian organic vision of the Old Testament covenant, the transformative vision of the Old Testament
prophets, and most significantly, the liberating and empowering vision of what the Gospels call the "kingdom of God." The
relational and empowering vision of both Jesus and St. Paul
struggled to hold its own amid the enduring power of patriar-

---

[5] Employing the rational mind to work things out by the power of
reason—instrumental reason—seems to have been initially a by-product of
the Agricultural Revolution reaching its first philosophical articulation in
the writings of Plato, further refined by Aristotle, and more recently associated with the French philosopher René Descartes.

chal rationality, but it did survive—and even flourished—until
the fourth century when the Roman emperor Constantine seriously jeopardized the subversive Christian vision. From that
time on, the Christian church acquiesced more and more to the
culture and demands of empire. Scripture scholar Wes Howard-Brook (2016) captures unambiguously what was transpir-
ing in the title of his book: *Empire Baptized: How the Church
Embraced What Jesus Rejected.*

Our Deviant Anthropology

Thus we complete the critique of our inherited anthropology,
the one that is so much taken for granted in our time and is
considered to be foundational to education, social policy, economics, politics, and religion throughout the modern world.
This anthropology is characterized by five key features:

- *Individual autonomy.* Human uniqueness is postulated
  on one's ability to stand on one's own feet, irrespective
  of, and apart from, all others. Ideally, each person should
  strive to become a "lone ranger," guaranteeing the best
  chance of winning in a fiercely competitive world and
  the best hope of individual salvation at the end of life's
  journey.
- *Ensoulment.* Aristotle does acknowledge a kind of
  soul in both plants and animals. However, the ensoulment of the human is superior to any other organic
  creature. This makes the human closer to God and
  endows humans with a God-given authority to lord
  it over everything else in creation. In secular terms, it
  translates into the neo-Darwinian survival of the fittest.
- *Separateness.* Aristotle sought to liberate humans from
  their enmeshment in the natural world, and Christianity has consistently encouraged its followers to flee the

world and not be too immersed in it. Ideally, therefore, the human must be over against, and superior to, everything that belongs to the natural realm, despite the fact that Christianity has also strongly endorsed the notion of following the natural law.

- *Rationality*. I have already highlighted this issue in describing Aristotelian anthropology. The ideal human works things out through the power of reason, through the medium of rational analysis and debate; Greek metaphysics provides the resources best suited for this enterprise.

- *Personal uniqueness*, which is defined by our differences from every other organism and every other entity, requiring us to mold and model our way of being in the world, in accordance with the four points listed above. Inadvertently, humans spend much of their time seeking to mold God (and Jesus) in our own image and likeness, using unexamined phrases such as, "A personal relationship with God, Jesus, Allah," and so on.

What is particularly disturbing is the naivety with which we collude with such an oppressive ideology. This way of being human is so inscribed in every sphere of life, it will take a momentous revolution to dislodge it. Indeed, it may not be an exaggeration to suggest—as Leakey and Lewin (1996) did many years ago—that we are now so disconnected from our true evolutionary purpose that we have effectively become the sixth extinction.[6] In other words, it

---

[6] Over the past 450 million years, life on Earth has been devastated by five mass extinction events that are widely recognized by geologists. Leakey and Lewin (1996) claim that we humans and our reckless environmental behavior constitute the sixth major extinction, the geographical and environmental details of which are outlined by *New York Times* scientific journalist Elizabeth Kolbert (2014). Currently, Dr. David Bond of the University

would appear that we are irretrievably sliding down the slope of self-destruction.

If this is true—and I suspect it is—then neither I nor any other force can reverse our plight. So why write this book at all? I do so for the following reasons:

- To help make sense of what is happening for those seeking an alternative way of being in the world.
- To invite a sense of realism in the face of catastrophe, when most political and religious leaders seem to be in a state of total denial.
- To facilitate death with dignity for those who seek to rise above the denial and rationalization of our plight.
- To offer realistic hope, along the lines suggested by the late Vaclav Havel, former president of the Czech Republic: Hope is definitely not the same thing as optimism. It is not the conviction that something will turn out well, but the certainty that something makes sense, regardless of how it turns out.

Hope

Beyond the Disconnect!

Faced with a world that seems to have betrayed our deep sacred inheritance, we are left with a disturbing sense of anomie and alienation that we often cover over with the false allurements of consumerism, hedonism, seductive power, or devotional religiosity. Neither God nor the universe ever intended us to live like this. We are in danger of betraying our true greatness. Not merely does it undermine our true human worth, but as I shall indicate throughout the rest of this book,

---

of Hull (in the United Kingdom) is considered an international authority on this research; several of his scientific papers can be accessed online.

it creates a disconnect from the rest of creation that is proving highly destructive in our time—for humans and planet alike.

So many people desire a new vision for the future! Some see it in technology, others in networking facilitated by mass communication. Others still see it in a new cosmology (popularly known as the New Story), while religions and churches hope for some kind of a religious revival. But without a renewed anthropology, one wonders how far any of these aspirations can go. The theory of original sin is attractive because it helps to make some sense of a flawed condition that keeps us from reaching our true greatness, but as I indicate in these opening chapters, our naming of that deficiency is itself based on a flawed anthropology. We need to ground our hope in an alternative vision, a more ancient anthropological narrative, imbued with creative, sacred, earthy, and integral meaning. Let's move ahead with that empowering exploration.

3

Toward an Alternative Anthropology

*A theology of embodiment mistrusts all abstract spiri-
tuality which is dissociated from the body, life, earth,
and social relationships. It trusts all embodiment which
speaks from a concrete, involved spirit, moved by eros
and related to the cosmos.*

—Elizabeth Moltmann-Wendel

For many fundamentalist Christians it all begins two thousand years ago. That is when Jesus came, when redemption was inaugurated, when the power of the resurrection re-created our world into God's new domain of power and glory. What happened before that axial moment of two thousand years ago is deemed to be of little or no importance. It can readily be ignored and forgotten. For those who cannot do that, hopefully some day they will see the light of Christ and cease wasting time and energy on futile nostalgic speculation.

As indicated in previous chapters, this shortsighted approach, based on a reductionistic time frame, has left us with a grossly distorted, flawed understanding of our humanity. Nothing short of divine intervention can rectify our irredeemably flawed condition. We have inherited a dysfunctional anthropology that some would claim is so perverse and corrupted it just cannot be reframed or redeemed. I claim, however, that it can be recontextualized and reframed anew, but admittedly to a degree that leaves the current paradigm in shatters. The present chapter sets out the alternative anthropology.

Throughout this chapter I use a two-pronged approach:

- First, I resituate the human species within the cosmic, planetary web of life, claiming that we are a derived species, evolving out of all the other life contexts that constitute the cosmic-planetary creation to which we belong. I claim that it is our contextual belonging, not our superior status, that constitutes our true nature.
- Second, in terms of the human story itself, I adopt the contemporary evolutionary trajectory that the study of paleontology (human origins) provides, a story of some 7 million years for the proto-human, and one of at least 3 million years for our status as fully human creatures (*Homo*). This horizon is vastly enlarged compared with the reductionistic view outlined in chapter 2. More significantly, it evidences a highly creative human being rather than the flawed creature who has left us with the distorted anthropology of recent millennia.

A New Cosmology

Let's begin with the cosmic context. All the major religions have adopted—and still adhere to—a three-tier universe, consisting of heaven above, the underworld (hell or Hades) beneath, and the earth in-between. We are dealing with a kind of geographical ideology, with everything above being ultra-real, everything beneath deemed to be problematic and unreliable, and the in-between earth awaiting its hour of liberation in which it will be enveloped by the heavenly realm above. While many people know that such a worldview has been seriously discredited, they struggle to identify a meaningful alternative. Such are the daily demands of survival that millions can't afford to think about such lofty matters. It is encouraging, however, to encounter a gradual awakening in which more and more people are realizing that we belong to something much more elaborate and ornate, something that can impact our lives for renewed meaning, growth, and progress.

This perception that we belong to something much greater and more complex than ourselves is the crucial issue here. Many years ago, the philosopher-cum-scientist Carl Sagan asserted, *The cosmos is within us. We are made of star-stuff. We are a way for the universe to know itself.* The missionary Filipino priest Benigno P. Beltran, fascinated by the ensuing visionary challenge, has written, "Science has given me tremendous opportunities for worship and gratitude. Science has deepened my appreciation of the scope of divine purpose and providence because of its discoveries in the realms of the immense and the infinitesimal, and its explanations of complexity and emergence" (Beltran 2012, 184). The ancient rootedness of this cosmic sense of awakening is captivated in this cryptic statement of the renowned physicist Stephen Hawking: "We are the product of quantum fluctuations in the very early universe."[1]

A new universal consciousness characterizes our time, awakening a novel search for meaning on a transnational, global scale. Ever before humans walked on the moon in 1969, scientists, philosophers, psychologists, and religionists were awakening to an expansive new horizon of meaning. In a moment of mystical intuition, Ernst Straus remarked to one of his assistants, "What really interests me is whether God had any choice in the creation of the world." The British mathematician

---

[1] www.hawking.org.uk/the-origin-of-the-universe.html.

James Jeans expressed it in these words: "The universe begins to look more like a great thought than a great machine. Mind no longer appears to be an accidental intruder into the realm of matter. We are beginning to suspect that we ought rather to hail it as the creator and governor of this realm" (1930, 137).

Millions of people today are growing up internally imbued with this cosmic wholeness. Most of us don't know what to do with it, and therefore, preoccupied with daily survival, tend to suppress this awakening wisdom. Those who do take it to heart, and it seems to be largely elderly people, go through a range of personal and psychic adjustments. Some give up inherited religion; others take on religion for the first time. Some make it a lifelong personal search; others opt for an intellectual elaboration, as we see with the University of the Third Age in the United States.

At the other end of the age spectrum, among younger people, the mystical-type awakening that happens during school years or early adulthood usually yields pride of place to the cultural compulsiveness to get a job and make money. When this same group, however, is confronted by a YouTube presentation of Stephen Hawking, Michio Kaku, Brian Cox, or the Dalai Lama, they detect a resonance, however fleetingly. Some will run with it; others won't.

In terms of the present book I wish to suggest that this inner cosmic resonance is very ancient, deeply inscribed in the human psyche, and foundational to the recovery of human creativity, a topic of central importance in these reflections. As I indicate in later chapters, the derogatory dismissal of our ancient ancestors as primitive, barbaric, and narrowly tribalistic results in a grossly distorted mode of understanding. They certainly did not understand and comprehend the world as we do today, but they experienced an immersion in the organic, cosmic web of life that we have long lost, and I wish to suggest we are all the poorer for it.

Our growing contemporary fascination with quantum physics and the new cosmology is not entirely new. We are reconnecting—or more accurately, we are being reconnected— with a deep ancient wisdom we have known intuitively for not merely thousands but some millions of years. And that ancient wisdom is not just about novel ways of understanding the creation around us. More importantly for the present work, it is the aperture that provides insight into our ancient incarnational soul, illuminating for us deeper dimensions of our humanity, long suppressed and undermined. The desire to recover—and reconnect with—our ancient past is central to the incarnational spirituality being explored in the present work.

What I am describing here is not merely a new emotional curiosity and intellectual fascination about the world in which we live; rather I am suggesting that a growing sense of cosmic "aliveness" is changing our very makeup as human beings. While biologically little seems to have changed throughout our two-hundred-thousand-year existence as *Homo sapiens*, internally (at the psychic and spiritual levels) dramatic shifts are happening within and among us, begetting what is essentially a new species. Beyond our anthropocentric superiority toward all other life forms, and a kind of dysfunctional loneliness that often accompanies such dualistic splitting, we are evolving a new consciousness of how intimately interconnected we are with the organic web of creation, and that our flourishing into fuller being is not possible without a deeper integration of our earthiness and cosmic organicity.

Belonging to the Gaian Web

The ensuing integration, with the multifaceted dimensions of our being and becoming, will need to begin with a fresh appreciation of what it means to be Earthlings. Many among us still suffer from the religious dismissal of our earthly status as a distraction from the things of heaven, and the promised fulfillment in a life hereafter. How to be at home within the living Earth itself and encounter therein that enduring mystery we call God will be for many of us the beginning of the new integration I am highlighting.

I wish to suggest that the outstanding scientific discovery of the twentieth century is not television or computer technology but rather *the complexity of the land itself as a living organism, and our convivial relationship to it as Earthlings.* Only those who know much about planet Earth can appreciate how little we actually do know. The Earth is seen as a living entity, a complex and intricately creative phenomenon. Once we truly grasp the organic reality of our "alive" planet and its physiology, our entire worldview and our embodied identity are bound to change profoundly—despite the fact that social, political, economic, and even religious forces will fiercely oppose such claims.

Gaia theory is a compelling new way of understanding life on our planet. The theory posits that the organic and inorganic components of planet Earth have evolved together as a single living, self-regulating system. It suggests that this living system has automatically controlled global temperature, atmospheric content, ocean salinity, and other factors, maintaining its own habitability. The theory was first popularized in the 1970s by British researcher James Lovelock (1979; 1988), and since then has been critically reviewed by a range of scientists, some highly dismissive, but a substantial number (predominantly from a biology background) applauding this Gaian perspective.

Somewhat similar to a human body's immune system, the Earth body is endowed with an inner wisdom that maintains conditions suitable for the Earth's own survival. Air (atmosphere), water (hydrosphere), earth (geosphere or pedosphere), and life (biosphere) interact to form a single evolving dynamism capable of maintaining environmental conditions consistent with life. In this respect, the living system of Earth may be compared to the immune system of any individual organism, regulating body temperature, blood salinity, and so on. So, for instance, even though the luminosity of the sun—the Earth's heat source—has increased by about 30 percent since life began almost 4 billion years ago, the living system has responded as a whole to maintain temperatures at levels suitable for life.

Our earth-embodiment, informed by the insights of the Gaia theory, suggests a complex and intelligent organic process that has direction and purpose deeply inscribed in its daily workings. *Process* is the crucial word here, the dynamic flow of which manifests a creative strategy, poorly understood and inadequately explained by conventional mechanistic science.

The New Biology

Even our status as biological organisms is undergoing evolutionary transformations, still poorly understood within biological science itself. In the past two hundred years, biology has undergone two significant evolutionary shifts. First was the work of Charles Darwin highlighted in his 1859 publication *On the Origin of Species* (see the valuable theological overview by Johnson 2015), and second was the "modern synthesis" that began in the 1920s and 1930s. The following are some of the key features of the modern synthesis, dated approximately from 1930 to 1970:

- The genome is always a well-organized library of genes.
- Genes usually have single functions that have been specifically honed by powerful natural selection.
- Species are finely adjusted to their ecological circumstances due to efficient adaptive adjustment of biochemical functions.

- The durable units of evolution are species, and within them the organisms, organs, cells, and molecules that are characteristic of the species.
- Given the adaptive nature of each organism and cell, their machinery can be modeled using principles of efficient design.

The new biology knits together genomics, bioinformatics, evolutionary genetics, and other such general-purpose tools to supply novel explanations for the paradoxes that undermined modernist biology. Because the genome is a complex and shifting patchwork, subject to many evolutionary and biochemical constraints and pressures, simple models of cellular or organismal function will often fail. Genomes can change rapidly due to selection mechanisms operating on multiple levels simultaneously, as well as the processes of transposition, mutation, and recombination.

The fundamental landscape of biology is undergoing a major upheaval. We cannot assume fixed relationships between structures and functions. As with other fields of contemporary research, this more fluid, evolutionary, dynamic approach evidences creative foundations to our being and becoming. We are creatures whose essential nature is better understood as that of an evolving process, rather than biological end-products. We are open-ended systems forever adjusting to new evolutionary imperatives. Fixity and stasis are no longer useful resources for growth and development. (For more on the new biology, see Sapp 2003; Rose & Oakley 2007; Church 2014.)

The Neglected Human Story

The psychologist Carl G. Jung wrote, "Our difficulties, neurotic, psychotic, psychopathic, or otherwise, come from losing contact with our instincts, with the age-old unforgotten wisdom stored up in us" (see Hull & Jacobi 1978, 76). More precisely, Jungian scholar Anthony Stevens chronicles this ancient psychic rootedness when he writes, "Where contemporary circumstances permit the archetypal needs of the two-million-year-old to be fulfilled, the result is that form of psychic adjustment we call health, but where contemporary circumstances frustrate the archetypal needs of the two-million-year-old, the result is maladjustment and illness" (Stevens 1993, xiv). For Stevens and many other Jungians, the archetypal is the antidote to the mechanistic, the rational, and the literal, with an anciently rooted wisdom largely unknown to contemporary human discourse.

As humans enter more deeply into the enlarged creation story that intrigues the contemporary mind and spirit—at the cosmic, planetary, and biological levels (briefly outlined above)—inevitably humans suspect that their conventional human story is deficient on several fronts. Our inherited anthropology lacks the grandeur that awakens deep within. As a result, we seek something much bigger, deeper, and more organically connected with the wider web of life. Paleontology—the study of human origins—opens a window into our deep past, with vast promise for transformative hope and meaning.

Consider the following list provided by science correspondent Heather Pringle (2013). It offers a glimpse into ancient creative developments, identified according to the rigorous research criteria of modern science:

- 3.4 mya (million years ago): cut-marked animal bones from Dikika, Ethiopia
- 2.6 mya: flaked stone tools from Gona, Ethiopia
- 1.76 mya: Bifacial stone tools from Turkana, Kenya
- 1.00 mya: Use of fire, Winderwerk Cave, South Africa
- 500,000 ya (years ago): pointed stone instruments, used with wooden handle, from Kathu Pan1, South Africa

- 164,000 ya: Heat-treated stone stools from Pinnacle Point, South Africa
- 100,000–70,000 ya: Engraved ochre, Blombos Caves, Lesotho
- 43,000 ya: Flutes, from Geissenklosterle Cave, Germany
- 40,000 ya: Ice Age art in Europe

As far back as the fourth millennium BCE, our ancestors were experimenting with natural resources—not merely for functional survival but to articulate and express *an inner creative urge that already at that time was moving in an artistic direction*. I am not interested in the myth of the noble savage (falsely attributed to philosopher Jean-Jacques Rousseau), itself a confused projection of disconnected Earthlings (see Ellingson 2001). I am not interested in giving a nice twist to an otherwise primitive story. My goal is to recover a capacity for human creativity deeply inscribed in our ancient human story.

Jungian scholar Anthony Stevens delineates the larger horizon along these lines:

> Rather than restrict ourselves to historical parallels from the relatively recent Sumerian, Egyptian, Greek, Roman past, I would go back much further, back to the hunter-gatherer existence for which our psyches were formed, back to the archetypal foundations of all human experience, back to the hominid, mammalian, and reptilian ancestors who live on in the structures of our minds and brains. It is to discover within Jung's two-million-year-old person, a 140-million-year-old vertebrate, which supports our finite existence and animates our dreams. (1993, 25)

I ask the reader to keep in mind here the Christian claim that we are fundamentally a flawed, sinful species; I see little evidence for that as I delve deeply into our ancient past. To the contrary I see a species with a creative impulse suggesting a very different anthropological imperative, namely, that we are first and foremost the beneficiaries of an original blessing and not the victims of an original sin" (cf., Matthew Fox, 1984). For the rest of this chapter I want to highlight what human life looks like when we live out of the endowment of being originally blessed.

Becoming Human

When did we actually evolve as a distinctive human species? Our response to this question will determine how we view and understand the human as a creative and spiritual being (the subject of this book) and as an incarnational creature (the focus of an earlier work, O'Murchu 2017). The various stages of our evolution as understood in modern paleontology I outline in two former works (O'Murchu 2008; 2017) and therefore do not repeat the details here. The reader needs to keep in mind the current distinction between *Australopithecus* and *Homo*. The Australopithicines usually denote the proto-human, beginning with *Sahelanthropus tchadensis*, popularly known as Toumai (about 7 mya), down to Sediba (about 2 mya). *Homo* describes creatures deemed to be human rather than chimpanzee, characterized by a certain brain size, the ability to walk upright (bipedal), and the skilful use of stone tools; *Homo habilis* (c. 2.8 mya) is considered to be the oldest ancestor fulfilling these requirements.[2]

---

[2] Today, the study of human origins, particularly in the realm of deep time, moves at an unprecedented pace, with a quality of scientific rigor, parallel to other sciences. For an up-to-date account, see http://humanorigins. si.edu/research. See also Harari 2015; Stringer 2012.

Of the three features that define our status as humans—
brain size, bipedalism, and stone technology—I briefly refer to
the first two and elaborate at greater length on the evolution
of stone technology. This third feature, more than any other,
highlights the capacity for creativity being explored in the present work.

1. *Brain size.* Compared to the chimpanzee brain, the
human brain is larger, and certain brain regions have been particularly altered during human evolution. Most brain growth
of chimpanzees happens before birth, while the development of
the human brain happens after birth. The philosopher Aristotle
claims that of all the animals, humans possess a brain largest in
proportion to body size. Charles Darwin also believed that the
size of the human brain, proportionate to its body, outwits that
of either the gorilla or orangutan, indicative of higher intelligence levels.

Measurements of cranial capacity are rather crude indi-
cators, but they are all that we have. Anatomical studies of
H. erectus crania suggest a much lesser cranial capacity (850–
1290 cm^3) than those of Upper Paleolithic *H. sapiens* (1302–
1600 cm^3) and the *Neanderthals* (1200–1689 cm^3), with only a
short period of postnatal brain maturation in all human cases.

The study of brain mass exceeding that related to an animal's total body mass is called *encephalization*, and quantify-
ing encephalization has been argued to be directly related to
an animal's level of intelligence. Researchers working with the
supposition that early humans were scavengers tend to support the notion that humans only developed more sophisticated skills when we began to hunt and acquire meat. Such
adaptive behavior, and specifically the dietary improvements,
contributed to the larger brains, differentiating humans from
their primate ancestors.

2. *Bipedalism.* At least twelve distinct hypotheses exist
as to how and why bipedalism evolved in humans and also

some debate as to when it first surfaced. Bipedalism evolved well before the large human brain or the development of stone tools. *Homo erectus*—the upright person—has long been considered as the first of our species to walk upright about 2 mya. In the late 1970s Mary Leakey discovered a set of footprints in Laetoli (Northwest Tanzania) that scientists have dated to 3.7 mya, almost doubling the earlier date for humans walking upright. Then came the quantum leap in the early years of the twenty-first century, when detailed examination of the Toumai skull indicates that our oldest known ancestor of some 7 mya walked upright.

At the present time, there is no consensus on this matter. The ability to walk upright is still considered to be central evidence for what defines the human above and beyond the primate. All we can conclude is that the human-as-human has been around much longer than we initially thought, further augmenting the argument of this book: that human creativity is also much older than we have long assumed.

3. *Stone technology*. In 1949 the British physical anthropologist Kenneth P. Oakley published a short book titled *Man the Tool-Maker*. Based on what many today consider limited research, it nonetheless evoked a scholarly curiosity that led to the unearthing of human potentialities, largely unknown up until that time and now foundational to the creativity being explored in the present work. While much of the scholarly interest focuses on the functional value of such ancient stone tools—for digging, scraping, and especially for extracting meat from animal bones—there has been an enduring curiosity on possible underlying artistic motifs. For instance, Oakely describes a dark red jasperite pebble found at a South African archaeological site (Makapansgat Member 4) dated to around 3 million years ago. The pebble has a shape that is reminiscent of a humanoid face and was transported far from its site of origin, suggesting that it was, perhaps because of its suggestive

human likeness, valued by the (probably) Australopithecine hominin who found it.

John A. Gowlett (1984; 2011) of the University of Liverpool, UK, has discussed the necessity of the Acheulian toolmaker to see the outline of the tool "in the mind's eye" or to use a "visuospatial sketchpad." The creation of an Acheulian biface (a hand-axe worked on both sides) by *H. erectus* in East Africa (and, after 600,000 BCE, by *H. heidelbergensis*) involved, first, the choice of a stone with a correctly curved surface, followed by a series of actions that followed a defined set of instructions—a "virtual manual," memorized by demonstration and repetition. The instructions involved the formation of separate planes along different axes, minimizing the computational complexities required to create the three-dimensional finished product. Some skill and intelligence at work here!

The study of ancient stone technology took a quantum leap in the second decade of the twentieth century, albeit focusing largely on functional (as distinct from artistic) use. In 2010 a startling announcement was made: Two bones with stone-tool butchery marks dated at 2.6 mya had been found at the Dikika site in Ethiopia, pushing the earliest traces of meat eating nearly a million years earlier than previously known. This was also far earlier than the earliest *Homo* fossils. Does this mean *Australopithecus* was just picking up naturally sharp rocks to use as stone knives (as most researchers claim) or are we witnessing something of a more sophisticated, imaginative set of skills with possible artistic intent?

And scientific research continues to delve deeper for possible creative breakthroughs. In May 2015 the discovery of 3.3-million-year-old stone tools from the Lomekwi 3 site in Kenya was announced, pushing back the origin of stone toolmaking by seven hundred thousand years. Just two months earlier, in March 2015, a 2.8-million-year-old fossil mandible and teeth from the Ledi-Geraru research area in Ethiopia were uncovered; the jaw predates the previously known fossils of the *Homo* lineage by approximately four hundred thousand years. These fossils have not been assigned to a particular species of early *Homo*, but it is now well accepted that they are the earliest fossils of our genus.

In April 2016 *Scientific American* carried a lead story on the pioneering work of Dietrich Stout, professor of anthropology at Emory University in Atlanta. Seeking to replicate the stone-technology behavior of our ancient ancestors, Stout has set up a pioneering project working collaboratively with a team of neuroscientists to detect brain activity during prolonged sessions of stone "knapping" (Stout 2016). Consistently, the brain activity being recorded and observed evidences high levels of creativity, leading to the notion of what Colin Renfrew (2009) calls the *sapient mind*.

The Artistic Flair

This pioneering endeavor challenges and even undermines the long-held view among language researchers that human creativity (intelligence, imagination, intuition, etc.) was only possible after language evolved, approximately one hundred thousand years ago. Prior to that time, it has long been assumed that humans were no better than animals in our ability to perceive and comprehend. It is after language that the ingredients of human intelligence fall into place (we have long been told), and humans have slowly evolved the capacity to engage their environment in more intelligently informed ways. This view could be described as the *restrictive language hypothesis*.

Ever since Kenneth Oakley's suggestion that our ancient toolmakers were endowed with an intelligent—and even artistic—flair, the restrictive language hypothesis is no longer defensible. Indeed, as neuro-anthropologist Terence Deacon (1997) indicates, language does not mark the beginning of more advanced human intelligibility, incorporating human creativity and a capacity for symbolism, but rather is the outcome of a species that has been portraying such creativity over several thousand years, thus cocreating the critical evolutionary threshold that leads to language as we understand it today.

To date the oldest evidence for our human artistic flair tends to be traced to Lower Paleolithic times. Two discoveries are frequently cited: the Venus of Berekhat Ram (c. 500,000–230,000 BCE) and the Venus of Tan-Tan (c. 500,000–200,000 BCE), generally considered to be the products of our Neanderthal ancestors. Most scholars consider the oldest known art in the world to be the Bhimbetka Petroglyphs, ten cupules and a groove, discovered in the quartzite auditorium rock shelter at Bhimbetka in Madhya Pradesh, Central India, dating to at least 290,000 BCE.

Human creativity is much older and more insinuated into our evolutionary flourishing than we have ever suspected. *It is the long-repressed truth that now needs to be reclaimed* in an anthropological narrative that must overcome the primitive assumptions to which science and religion have been wedded for far too long. Fortunately, it is more rigorous science itself that invites us to such daring new horizons, like that of the scholar of comparative studies, Christopher Collins (2013), who explores the cognitive skills that predate language and writing. These include the brain's capacity to perceive the visible world, store its images, and retrieve them later to form simulated mental events. Long before humans could share stories through speech, they perceived, remembered, and imagined their world in a range of preverbal narratives.

As indicated above, since April 2015 the oldest dating for ancient stone technology is that of 3.3 mya. We can no longer assume that this was merely a functional endeavor, serving rational and pragmatic purposes. Although, to date, we have no concrete evidence for an artistic dimension, the research of

Dietrich Stout and others requires us to keep open the possibility—even the likelihood—that in time such evidence will be forthcoming. In our species the capacity for creativity seems considerably older than we currently assume.

From a religious perspective, however, it is not merely the challenge of acknowledging this underlying artistic, creative capacity in terms of deep time, but to accept what has been thoroughly researched and extensively verified throughout the twentieth century, namely Ice Age / Paleolithic art. Nowhere is our ancient wisdom more impressive than in the rich reservoirs of Paleolithic art and its related expressions in places as diverse as Europe, Australia, Indonesia, and southern Africa (Cook 2013; Lewis-Williams, 2002). The cave at Lascaux (discovered in 1940) and that of Chauvet-Pont-d'Arc (discovered in 1994)—both in Southern France—provide the finest examples of Ice Age art.[3] Similar finds have been replicated elsewhere, notably in Australia, southern Africa, and most recently (2014) in Indonesia.

Ice Age Art

From the time of their first discovery, a number of theories have evolved to explain the meaning of Ice Age art. The first was "art for art's sake," suggesting that our ancient ancestors were endowed with a strong artistic flair—an idealiza-

---

[3] Access to both sites is severely restricted owing to the experience at Lascaux, whereby the admission of visitors on a large scale led to the growth of mould on the walls that damaged the art in places. A facsimile of Chauvet Cave, on the model of the so-called "Faux Lascaux," was opened to the general public on April 25, 2015. It is the largest cave replica ever built worldwide, ten times bigger than the Lascaux facsimile. The art is reproduced full-size in a condensed representation of the underground environment. Visitors' senses are stimulated by the same sensations of silence, darkness, temperature, humidity, and acoustics, carefully reproduced to captivate something of the foundational experience of the original participants.

tion dismissed by most researchers, but as argued throughout this book, an ancient endowment deserving a far more serious discernment. Next came the idea, propagated by Henri Brueil, that the images support the practice of sympathetic magic so that the hunters would have success in the hunt—based on ethnological research, reinforced by the fact that existing hunter-gatherers were producing rock art into the late nineteenth century. However, many of the animals depicted on the caves were not those hunted by humans at the time. Then there is the structuralist approach (founded by Claude Lévi-Strauss) viewing the animals as mythic totems, a theory that never gained much credibility among researchers.

A new slant in archaeology, led by Andre Leroi-Gorham, relied on the positioning of the paintings and their placement in relation to one another, studying the frequency of their appearance. This led to the identification of recurring themes, one of which is the *shamanistic motif.* Is rock art related to shamanistic rites? Could it be illustrative of shamanistic rituals? The French prehistorian Jean Clottes, in collaboration with South African anthropologist David Lewis-Williams (Clottes & Lewis-Williams 1998), believes that the artwork is the outcome of people in trance states, induced by psychotropics along with dancing, drumming, and fasting. This is currently the leading theory—although the case has not been made in a definitive manner and the mystery of the cave art remains.

Few can deny that the emergence of cave art some 40,000 years ago marked a new threshold in the evolution of human consciousness. The capacity for symbolic expression reached novel heights of sophistication and creativity. To delve into this mystery requires an ability to explore the prehistory of the mind and to trace developmental stages that stretch much further back than we have heretofore considered. The Blombos caves in Lesotho (southern Africa) confirm that people wore decorated and symbolic jewelry possibly as far back as 90,000 years ago. Artifacts of artistic flair have been found in many parts of the African subcontinent, predating the major European and Australian finds (cf. *Science Daily*, Aug. 27, 2009), the oldest to date being the decorated shellfish of Pinnacle Point (South Africa)—dated at 164,000 years ago.[4]

Those who have had the good fortune to stand in front of Paleolithic cave paintings frequently experience awe and reverence. Of particular intrigue are the *therianthropes* with the composite structure of both human and animal. Several are in similar postures, with one leg raised in what appears to be a dance movement. These have horned animal heads on human bodies with their sexual organs prominent, often ithyphallic. In the shaft at Lascaux, we see a human body with a bird head. There is also an ivory statue of a lion-man. The rhinoceros figure in the Chauvet cave also seems to carry shamanic significance. These mysterious envoys have been regarded as masked shamans or as divine animal masters, as totems, as personifications of the forces of nature, and as archetypes of the ancestors that reach back before humans were separated from

---

[4] Recent excavations, most revealingly in South African caves, have provided significant insight into symbolic activity, including the use of color, engraving of patterns, bone technology and bead-making, dating from some 164,000 years ago (Henshilwood et al. 2011; Marean et al. 2007). The oldest known use of ochre is also dated at 164,000 years ago, from a South African coastal site, Pinnacle Point, where fifty-seven pigment pieces were found (Marean et al. 2007). At least ten of the pieces had been ground or scraped; these had been deliberately selected as the most intensely red pigments. Neanderthals also used charcoal in a similar manner. These observations suggest the use of pigment for body decoration or camouflage by European Neanderthals—at least 60,000 years ago—apparently with a preference for black.

the animals. We seem to be standing at a cosmic threshold that unites animals and humans in a deep archetypal symbiosis, reconnecting us with a time when we were as yet undifferentiated from the powers of nature. Additionally, religious scholar Justin Jeffcoat Schedtler (2017, 56) notes that epigraphic and archaeological research into the ancient Mother Goddess frequently depicts her surrounded by animals.

Animals feature extensively in the paintings, indicating a fascination that clearly transcends issues related to fertility or the hunt. It has also been suggested that people of the time believed that animal spirits were there inside the walls, half ready to come out. Painting the missing outlines drew forth the animal-spirit, giving more direct access to their spiritual power. This theory has obvious associations with the possibility of shamanism and the celebration of shamanic rituals, already noted above (more in Lewis-Williams 2002), and requires us to hold open a range of other spiritual and ritualistic possibilities that time may yet illuminate.

Often associated with the European Ice Age art in the upper Paleolithic period are the Venus statuettes. The first representation was discovered about 1864 by the Marquis de Vibraye in the Dordogne region of France. The famous Venus of Willendorf was excavated in 1908 in the Danube Valley in Austria. Since then, hundreds of similar figurines have been discovered from the Pyrenees to the plains of Siberia. To the modern viewer, some of the images look quite grotesque, obese, and exaggerated. Many interpreters agree that the affirmation of female fertility is a central motif. More controversially, some link the figurines with the possible worship of a female divine embodiment known as the Great Goddess (more in Reid-Bowen 2007). The possible implications for revisioning a creative understanding of God (Deity) are substantial and are reviewed in a later chapter.

Greek and Christian Distortions

To the ancient Greeks, the concept of a creator and of creativity implied freedom of action, but art carried a more confined significance, subject to certain laws and rules. Art (in Greek, *techne,* root word for technique and technology) was the making of things according to specified rules. It contained no creativity, and it would have been—in the Greeks' view—a bad state of affairs if it had. The Romans adopted a more liberal stance: artists shared with poets the qualities of imagination and inspiration and therefore were not expected to abide by rules to the same degree as the Greeks.

In the ancient cultures of Greece and Rome, people believed that creativity belonged to a divine attendant spirit that influenced human beings from a divine source that could neither be comprehended nor explained in a rational way. The Greeks often referred to these divine attendant spirits of creativity as *daemons.* Socrates famously believed that he had a daemon that spoke to him from afar. The Romans held similar views for which they used the notion of *genius,* not necessarily somebody with remarkable intelligence, but rather a spirit-force of divine magical quality, which, for example, could inhabit the walls of an artist's studio, and that would come out and invisibly assist in the artistic endeavor, giving shape and substance to the artist's work.

This understanding of art was premised on the belief that nature is perfect and subject to laws that humans should respect and obey, and without which human potential will not produce to its optimum level. The artist was a discoverer, not an inventor. The sole exception to this Greek view was poetry. The poet *created* something essentially new, while the artist merely *imitated.* And the poet, unlike the artist, was not bound by laws.

A fundamental change, however, came in the Christian period: *creatio* came to designate God's act of "creation from nothing" (*creatio ex nihilo*). *Creatio* thus took on a different meaning than *facere* (to make), the term more widely used to describe acts of human genius. The Middle Ages, however, went even further than antiquity when they revoked poetry's exceptional status, viewing it as an artistic craft and not creativity in the strict sense.

All the great religions witness to a range of creative expressions through art, music, sculpture, and architecture. And from the fourth century onward we evidence the same creative orientation within Christianity. Consider Christian church structure—with its cross-shaped nave and transept, its wealth of sign and symbol, and story in stained glass, stone, and wood carving—and the very design of the church building itself (which was called, in preliterate society, "the poor people's Bible," because it filled the heart and mind with images, colors, and shapes that spoke of divine realities). Art found diffuse expression in medieval and Renaissance painting, sculpture, and music—used as vehicles for expressing the glory of God. In the Baroque era, composers such as Bach made notations on their musical scores: *Soli gloria deo* (glory to God alone). Art and religion shared a common aspiration.

We must also include the wonderful iconography of the Greek and Russian Orthodox communities. Think of the way Native American art and animistic African art mirror their belief systems. However, with the Enlightenment, art and religion began to split apart in European and Western culture, so that even a poet as deeply in tune with the natural and supernatural worlds as Gerard Manley Hopkins felt compelled, after entering the Jesuit order, to burn his early work, a sacrifice he labeled "the slaughter of the innocents." For seven years thereafter Hopkins rigorously disciplined himself, attempting in his priestly role to worship and serve God apart from poetry until his religious superior hinted in his hearing that 'someone" ought to write a poem about the wreck of the ship *Deutschland*. Hopkins's poetic flair took off once more with renewed vigor.

Subverted Creativity

The present chapter has highlighted two main strands of subverted human creativity:

- *Humanity's evolving story retraced into deep time*— covering not merely thousands but millions of years— exhibiting a growing body of creative endeavor, especially through ancient stonework. Scientifically rigorous and thoroughly researched, these ancient findings must now become an integral part of anthropology and must also be included in our understanding of what constitutes the human condition, whether in politics, economics, social policy, or religion.
- *The very recent emphasis on rationality and the use of reason as the key qualities of being authentically human.* Consequently, the other faculties of imagination, intuition, and the creative impulse were deemed to be inferior and considered a threat to the evolution of more robust, patriarchal humanism. Such a view is no longer sustainable.

In the present chapter I have sought to recapture and articulate afresh an enduring creative impulse that has characterized the human species for at least 3 million years. Hidden within that creative urge were cosmic and planetary horizons that rational philosophy and science brutally subverted. Paradoxically, it is science itself—in the form of quantum physics, new cosmology, the new biology, and contemporary ecology— that is leading the way in a new cultural and spiritual revival, redefining our identity as human beings and as creatures of divine benevolence.

The retrieval of this artistic flair also carries religious and ethical implications, none more weighty than our need to readdress the prevailing myth of original sin. While not doubting or denying our capacity to get things wrong, we must wrestle afresh with our ancient capacity to get things right and beautify our world with a range of artistic endowments. Perhaps someday when we take the daring risk of prioritizing our creative side and adopting it as the basis for our religion, spirituality, and theology, we will realize an alternative way of serving both God and our created world.

Central to this suggested expansive horizon is the challenge to outgrow the dualistic splitting that has defined us as humans for far too long. Of particular significance is our status as Earthlings, exhibiting a convivial relationship with the living Earth itself—not as an object to be conquered and controlled—but rather as the organic nexus that defines and sustains every aspect of our human identity. To that dimension we now turn our attention.

4

Sacredness and the Earth

*The human body is not a closed or static object, but an
open, unfinished entity utterly entwined with the soils,
waters, and winds that move through it—a wild crea
ture whose life is contingent upon the multiple other
lives that surround it, and the shifting flows that surge
through it.*

—David Abram

Our ancient creativity haunts several fields of contemporary
study and research. Two features are particularly challenging
and are the focus of this chapter: *spirituality* and *earthiness*. All
creativity arises from deep within the human psyche and can be
explained through a range of cultural insights explored through
psychology, anthropology, and the study of human behavior in
general. Spirituality—often confused with religion—tends not
to be included, a neglected area that seems to me at the center
of a more comprehensive overview of human creativity.

Second comes the more formidable challenge to come
to terms with our groundedness in the Earth itself—and our
significance as Earthlings—as foundational to the creativity I

am exploring throughout this book. It is also in and through our *earthiness* that we integrate the spiritual vitality of human existence. We are engaging a complex process of investigation and discernment that challenges some of our most enduring cultural assumptions, particularly the dualistic split between the sacred and the secular.

If the caves associated with Ice Age art were sites for various shamanic rites, then we need to probe further and ask what sense of sacredness infused and animated such religious behavior. Both Jean Clottes and David Lewis-Williams (Clottes & Lewis-Williams 1998) invite us to consider a ritualistic culture in which people experienced a tangible sense of connection with a spiritual life force. They observe that stenciled hand prints, produced by placing a hand on the wall and blowing pigment around it and between the fingers, are found throughout world rock art, in European caves and on rocks from Australia, America, and South Africa. Lewis-Williams (2002) suggests that we should not view the drawings as the work of individual artists but more likely a communal endeavor related to sacred ritual.

Are we dealing with some ancient form of animism, pagan worship, or something more elusive? Is there a spirit connection that contemporary religion may not be able to discern or comprehend, simply because our religious presuppositions cannot entertain such a possibility? The anthropologist views the evolution of religion differently, noting first that all the major religions we know today emerged in the wake of the Agricultural Revolution (c. ten thousand years ago), and second that patriarchal influences are very much at the fore of such emergence. Consequently, the supernatural is a transcendent force, divorced from and dualistically opposed to the natural world, and authentic religious wisdom has to be subjected to the bar of reason. Consequently, all the great religions display varying degrees of ambivalence around shamanism and various articulations of mystical experiences and tend to suppress, and even ridicule, forms of spirituality closely aligned with the natural world.

In the present chapter I want to run with the notion that Ice Age cave art has something to do with the spiritual force we name as *Spirit-power*, and I take the liberty of suggesting that our ancestors of some forty thousand years ago were deeply imbued with what might best be called *Spirit-consciousness*. Formal religion as we know it today did not exist at that time, yet people behaved with levels of spiritual awareness and ritual engagement that defy much of the religiosity of later millennia. Levels of collaboration with the divine Spirit and an ensuing integrated set of spiritual values may well be ancient creative resources that are virtually impossible to retrieve in contemporary religious studies.

Enter the Great Spirit

One possible route to accessing this deep, ancient religious consciousness is to review the spirituality of our current indigenous / tribal / First Nations peoples. Such peoples exist in virtually every part of planet Earth today and have been the subject of anthropological research for well over one hundred years. Most of these tribal groups have never met each other and have rarely communicated, even with the means of contemporary information technology. Yet they all hold some remarkably similar religious beliefs, none more intriguing than their understanding of the divine life force as the Great Spirit. In a previous work (O'Murchu 2012) I examine this belief in substantial detail, the main insights of which I summarize in this chapter.

I find it strange that belief in the Great Spirit is known universally among tribal and indigenous peoples and yet has not been the subject of serious investigation. Such is the insidious nature of our prejudices that we tend to dismiss such beliefs as primitive and prerational—another form of ancient animism. Others regard the notion of the Great Spirit as the name Christian missionaries gave to the pagan Gods of unevangelized peoples. Even among indigenous peoples themselves, the notion of the Great Spirit seems to be poorly understood.

The following are some of the central features of this ancient belief:

1. We are dealing with a mystical, experiential perception, a visceral feeling of an energy force that permeates and informs everything in creation. As an energy form, however, it is subtle, pervasive, and infused with an inherent directionality toward meaning and purpose. Quantum physics is probably the only branch of the human sciences that illuminates this ancient understanding of energy-force (more in Schafer 2013). We can also draw on religious/philosophical precedents from the ancient Chinese notion of *chi* (see Kim 2011) and from the Vedic concept of *prana* (see McCaul 2007; Maehle 2012).

2. Therefore, the Great Spirit is not a *personal* Deity as understood in religions such as Judaism, Christianity, or Islam, nor does it involve worship of divine figureheads as in Hinduism and Sikhism. Researchers then leap to a totally false and superficial conclusion: we are dealing with a primitive, impersonal life force, perceived to be inferior to a personalized understanding of Deity. For indigenous peoples, the Great Spirit is neither personal nor impersonal. There is no dualistic splitting in this belief system. The Great Spirit may be described as *transpersonal*, in the sense that it embraces everything that constitutes personhood and yet transcends all our anthropomorphic reductionisms, and the several cultural projections whereby we are often—inadvertently—molding God in our own image and likeness. (For more on the Asian perspective, see Lee 1979, 109ff.)

3. How then do these ancient peoples know and relate to the Great Spirit? *Through the living Earth itself.* This is an insight of enormous significance, bypassed by several researchers and rarely understood in depth by indigenous peoples themselves. It is in and through our symbiotic relationship with the living Earth itself that we encounter and engage with the Great Spirit. Our earthiness may be understood as an umbilical cord through which is channeled the living energy of all creation (past, present, and future), the source and sustenance of which is the Great Spirit. *Our earthiness is the royal road to our holiness.* It is the anchor through which meaning is grounded and sustained for all areas of daily life, including our engagement with the sacred.

4. It is, therefore, our status as *Earthlings* that grounds us in this deeply intimate affiliation with the Great Spirit. Contrary to Christianity, we do not need to be ensouled by some divine intervention to become sacred, holy, or God-like. Our very earthiness already makes us God-like, or in the seminal intimations of the great Catholic theologian Karl Rahner, by nature we are inherently open to divine mystery. Our transpersonal understanding of God as person, therefore (see number 2 above), is mediated through our earthiness, or more accurately through our embeddedness in the cosmic web of life itself.

5. This immersion in the divine mystery to which we intimately belong should not be confused with *pantheism* (God has no meaning outside creation), nor with the frequently cited alternative of *panentheism* (God is in creation but not confined to it). We are dealing with a time-space understanding that knows no separation of a within and a without. This is the all-is-one experiential mode known to mystics of every age and culture. And like the mystics, indigenous peoples do not speculate about the nature, meaning, or essence of God; in fact, Christianity seems to be the only religion preoccupied with metaphysical distinctions. Indigenous peoples, ancient and

modern, *do not worship God*. Instead they strive to live in harmony with the Great Source; their often elaborate rituals serve the purpose of a more wholesome collaboration with Divine wisdom and should not be confused with the notion of worship as practiced in the other great religions.

6. Thus we arrive at a characteristic of indigenous peoples widely documented across planet Earth: *a unique and loving regard for the sacredness of the land*. Many tribal peoples have had painful and protracted experiences trying to reclaim their native lands, sometimes with the contradictory outcome of then reassigning sections of their land for commercial uses, largely if not totally alien to the spirit of their faith. The convivial relationship with the soil/land exhibited among indigenous peoples on a universal scale should be understood primarily in theological terms: the land is perceived to be the divine vehicle through which divine wisdom percolates into all forms of organic life, including that of the human.[1]

7. Mainline religions tend to be identified in terms of a *formal creed* (set of beliefs), an *ethical code*, and a *structure of worship*. Belief in the Great Spirit collapses all three into one foundational focus: the sacredness of the Earth itself. How that sacredness is upheld, protected, and promoted is what guides the belief in the Great Spirit. At times it feels like situational ethics: work it out as you go along. Yet the evidence shows strong communal bonds, ethical values, and profound respect for the Great Spirit, who can be awesome,

---

[1] The reader needs to keep in mind here the contemporary symbiotic relationship between planet Earth and the cosmos at large. Earth is energized by the cosmos (universe). Consequently, it would be more accurate to view the Great Spirit as the energizing, empowering force of the entire universe, with planet Earth as one derived aspect. I allude mainly to the Earth-dimension, because that is the aspect—if you wish, the grounding through which—Earthlings embark upon their spiritual growth and development in terms of faith in the Great Spirit.

fierce, and destructive, but in the end also benevolent and supportive of all life.

8. Finally, such belief should not be confused with *animism*, which conveys the notion of everything being endowed with a soul. The concept of ensoulment is unknown in the primordial experience of such indigenous faith. We do encounter various allusions to divine intervention, along lines that seem similar to divine ensoulment. In all probability this results from the influence of Christian or Muslim missionaries and occurs most frequently among African tribal peoples. Similarly, when we encounter a gendering of the Great Spirit into a leading patriarchal figurehead, in all probability we are once more evidencing external missionary influence. The Great Spirit transcends all anthropomorphic projections and should instead be viewed as a cosmic-planetary creative dynamism forever luring humans beyond their dualistic antagonism into more convivial relationships with the living Earth itself.

Our Earthy Sacredness

We have long associated sacredness with belief in a supreme being, luring us away from the sin and temptation of this earthly condition to the ultimate fulfillment of life in a trans-earthly, heavenly abode. Under the aegis of the patriarchal, father God, we lost sight of earth-sacredness, and to resolve the ensuing alienation, we sought to escape the proverbial "vale of tears" for an elusive happiness in a distant eternity. And we were indoctrinated into assuming that that was the true narrative, and the one that had sustained us throughout the long distant past.

Nothing could be further from the truth. This distant patriarchal figurehead, so hard to placate, is largely an invention of postagricultural times (less than ten thousand years old). The new mastery that the agriculturalists desired required, among other things, a patriarchal God-figure that would validate their every

wish. They enthroned him in the heavens and created a descending hierarchy of rulers who would represent him on Earth. At the
fore was the king and all the royal saviors who ensued thereafter.[2]

Thus we destroyed an earlier strand, almost impossible
to retrieve as the patriarchs attempted to wipe it out forever.
Mythological echoes abound of an Earth Mother Goddess
whose focus was an empowering, egalitarian nexus in which
both women and men played collaborative roles (more in Reid-
Bowen 2007). Usually dismissed as a fantasized nostalgia, its
recurring demand to be heard afresh and rehabilitated anew
petrifies the patriarchs even to this day. And it embodies a set
of egalitarian aspirations that are assumed to wreak anarchy
and havoc on Earth.

When we study Ice Age art and several other creative out-
lets as explored in chapter 3, we don't find much evidence for
such anarchy and havoc. To the contrary, we detect an organic,
interrelated symbiosis between species and planet, between the
human and the surrounding web of life. What was the prevailing consciousness of these earlier times? Dare I suggest that the
following quote from the contemporary physicist Lothar Schafer captivates a long-lost wisdom, imbued with an empowering
sense of creativity?

> When reality is an undivided wholeness, we aren't
> hemmed in by its infinity, but we belong to it. When
> the background of the universe is mind-like, we aren't
> alone in the universe, but the *cosmic spirit* is thinking
> with us. In your thoughts are divine thoughts. In your

---

[2] In the case of the Judeo-Christian story, particularly the Hebrew
Scripture (Old Testament), the historical representation of the ruling patriarchal God in the earthly king is dated to a mere one thousand years before
the Christian era. See the comprehensive overview of Howard-Brook 2010,
esp. 11–15.

kindness, divine kindness comes to the fore. And in the potential in you, the infinite divine potential is trying to express itself in the empirical world. Why it needs us, I have no idea. Perhaps the answer is that we are the *cosmic spirit* and the *cosmic spirit* is us. (2013, 215; emphasis added)

Is this how the religious adherents of the Great Spirit viewed reality? It certainly represents how the Great Spirit is understood today. The suggestion that we inhabit a mind-like universe is upheld by a wide range of physicists and cosmologists (see Davies 1993; Kafatos 2013; Chopra & Kafatos 2017). Is science reconnecting us with threads that have been destructively frayed by formal religions? Is our ancient creativity, itself an endowment of the Great Spirit, coming back to haunt us? And where do we find a theology and spirituality to sustain us in the pilgrimage of rediscovery? Hopefully, the present book is a contribution, however small, toward that end.

Faith in the Great Spirit therefore rests on one enduring assertion: *sacredness is*! We don't need to search for it in religions or anywhere else. It is staring us in the face; it irrupts all around us and within us, if only we could submit to its ambience. In these fantastic claims, there is no delusion of self or other. Belief in the Great Spirit does not deny the harsh truth that nature is red in tooth and claw. As a faith system, however, it embraces the paradox of pain and suffering, seeks to engage with it intelligibly (and creatively), and befriend it in those bewildering natural processes where nature needs its destructive elements to beget new breakthroughs.

The Judeo-Christian Land Ethic

At the heart of the covenant between God and the Jewish people is embeddedness in the land itself—not merely the reli-

gious/political entity known as the land of Israel, the subject of
prolonged violent rhetoric in the Hebrew Scripture, but rather
the land as a nourishing, sustaining, and creative resource. The
opening chapter of Genesis launches the earth as good, beautiful, and fruitful, in truth a land flowing with milk and honey
to reassure the bewildered people in their experience of exile
(see Exod. 3:8). And to ensure that all had access to the land's
fruitfulness, and that the fertility of the land itself would be
safeguarded by due rest, the notion of Jubilee evolved. The biblical description needs to be read against the background of an
agrarian culture, adopting something akin to a barter economy:

> Every seventh year you shall grant a remission of
> debts. And this is the manner of the remission: every
> creditor shall remit the claim that is held against a
> neighbor, not exacting it of a neighbor who is a mem-
> ber of the community, because the LORD's remission
> has been proclaimed. . . . There will, however, be no
> one in need among you, because the LORD is sure to
> bless you in the land that the LORD your God is giving
> you as a possession to occupy. (Deut. 15:1–4)

For the Hebrew people, the land is fundamentally sacred,
an intuition shared by several ancient cultures and largely hidden in the discourses of the great world religions. For instance,
the accounts of the early Israeli kibbutznik farmers all describe
the mystical relationship they maintained with the land, despite
being passionate rationalists and secularists. It all began to
change as the patriarchal influences sought out an imperial
territory that quickly assumed exclusive national identity as the
land of Israel, and as the Jews came to understand themselves
as a chosen people over against all others. It was then a short
step to the objectification and commodification of land, which
then becomes the target of violent acquisition and oppression.

The agrarian culture gives way to the imperial *polis* (city). Such anthropocentric abuse of the land (in the Hebrew context) seems to have resulted from Roman infiltration, reinforced by the Hellenistic preoccupation with individualism and the ownership of private property.

The disconnect—and consequent loss of integrated creativity—that over the past two millennia has become a universal phenomenon is well articulated by the philosopher David Abram:

> The pain, the sadness of this exile, is precisely the trace of what has been lost, the intimation of a forgotten intimacy. The narratives in Genesis remain deeply attuned to the animistic power of places, and it is this lingering power that lends such poignancy to the motifs of exodus and exile. . . . Eternity lies not in a separated heaven (the ancient Hebrews knew of no such realm) but in the promise of a future reconciliation on the earth. (Abram 1996, 196–97)

By the time Christianity evolves, the usurpation and commodification of the land is almost taken for granted. On closer scrutiny, however, we see a quite deliberate attempt at restoring an ecological equilibrium, so that people can engage with the land in more creative and sustainable ways. This claim is made primarily on the basis of the Gospel parables, many of which focus on land use (and abuse) as the catalyst for a new breakthrough.

In the time of Jesus the majority of the people lived on the land. It was the basis of their daily survival, not merely for food, but for a vast range of raw products used for building, clothing, and herbal cures. As with several indigenous people today, Jesus's contemporaries believed that the land owned them rather than they owning the land. But this organic, mystical relationship became ever more tenuous as the Romans piled on taxes to maintain the empire while the priestly aristocracy also extracted taxes for the maintenance of the temple. When the people could not pay, they began to do deals with rich landowners who often played "dirty games" pretending to favor the people while all the while robbing them of the primary source of their well-being.

The several parables dealing with landowners and vineyards—many of which seem to be authentically from Jesus himself—are actually subversive stories about the exploitation of land (Herzog 1994; van Eck 2016). Using a strategy very similar to Paulo Freire's "pedagogy of the oppressed," Jesus confronts both oppressors and oppressed with the glaring injustices of the prevailing socioeconomic system, seeking to conscientize and empower those victimized by the deviant power of their exploiters. For gospel empowerment the land is integral to holiness, growth, and flourishing. There can be no human creativity apart from the organic fecundity of the earth itself.

Unfortunately, the evangelists—the Gospel writers—seem to have missed this subversive thrust, partly due to translating the more proactive Aramaic that Jesus spoke into the literalized Greek of daily imperial discourse, as in the case of the parable of the Talents (Matt. 25:14–30). The latter sought out rational resolution for situations that were far from reasonable. The parables attempt a more subversive resolution to a range of precarious situations, which from the perspective of the little tradition (the poor) looked anything but rational. Moreover, the evangelists (or later interpreters) allegorize the original stories, stripping them of their cultural and theological destabilization, overspiritualizing them to a point where prophetic contestation is seriously undermined.

To illustrate the way parables have been displaced from their original intent—to the detriment of the creative relationship with the land—consider the seminal parable of the Late Night Visitor seeking hospitality (Luke 11:5–8):

> Jesus said to them, "Which of you, if you go to a friend at midnight, and tell him, 'Friend, lend me three loaves of bread, for a friend of mine has come to me from a journey, and I have nothing to set before him,' and he from within will answer and say, 'Don't bother me. The door is now shut, and my children are with me in bed. I can't get up and give it to you'? I tell you, although he will not rise and give it to him because he is his friend, yet because of his persistence, he will get up and give him as many as he needs."

In its foundational meaning this is a parable about *hospitality*, with an extensive range of meanings incorporating land in both its planetary and cosmic significance. Luke, however, allegorizes the parable, using it as a rationale for persistent prayer (see Luke 11:9–13). Undoubtedly, commentators old and modern have used parablelike stories to evangelize the reader (hearer) into a range of faith responses. The outcome, while spiritually meritorious, frequently undermines and even erodes the holistic (nondual) cultural vision, often embodying a theological breakthrough far more dynamic and empowering than the religiously flavored allegorization.

When dealing with the Christian gospel, three important distinctions need to be made between aspects of Jesus's parables:

1. The *Story*: The overt outline of the main characters and their impact upon each other.
2. The *Allegory*: Adapting the story to teach a religious spiritual truth (or virtue), e.g., how to relate rightly with God.

3. The *Parable*: Discerning the subtle elements that give
   the story a surplus of meaning, not transparent at first
   telling, and sometimes embodying multiple meanings
   of a subversive nature.

So, how is the story of the late-night visitor to be heard as a
parable?

In the Palestine of Jesus's time, people often preferred to
travel after dark in order to avoid the heat, and visitors would
commonly arrive unannounced. No matter what time of day
or night one arrives, the Jewish norms of hospitality require
that you attend to the person's need (Gen. 18:1–8; Heb. 13:2).
There is no question of refusing. For a host to be unable to
offer hospitality to a guest would be shameful; more importantly, it would bring shame not only on himself *but upon the
entire village*. A guest is a guest of the community, not just
of the individual, and to comply with cultural and religious
expectations, a guest must leave the village with a good feeling
about the hospitality offered not just by individuals but by the
village-as-community.

At night, food may not be as readily available, since bread
was baked in the morning to meet each day's anticipated needs.
Despite the practical difficulties, the village hospitality demands
that bread must be provided for the guest. So the host decides
to walk to his neighbor's house, knock on his door, and ask
him for three loaves of bread. This householder is also bound
by the expectations of cultural hospitality, and despite the great
inconvenience, he gets up and gives bread for the traveler.

We need to note carefully the subtle wisdom embedded in
many of the Gospel parables. In this case the central issue is
hospitality, but in parabolic terms it is about God's hospitality
to the people, obligating the people to exercise similar generosity, with the hidden impetus of global prolificacy. If the individuals don't provide bread for the traveler they are shamed

in the eyes of the (religious) culture, but so is the entire village (in the eyes of the wider culture but also in the eyes of God). In contemporary ecological terms, the *village* is the equivalent of the *bioregion*. And every bioregion is sustained by planet Earth, which in turn is upheld by the cosmic universe. In other words, the act of hospitality is not merely an interpersonal gesture of goodwill. It is an act of God-like hospitality embracing the bioregion, the earth, and the universe. It is the exposition and illumination of this expansive creative horizon that converts a simple story into a highly complex prophetic parable.

On Holy Ground

The convivial relationship with land and soil described in the present chapter is unknown to millions of Earth's inhabitants today. Those of us raised and reared in urban environments frequently are unacquainted with the organic creativity of the earth itself. Many of us live with a subverted sense of alienation having been expelled from the very womb that begot us. The mechanization, commodification, and globalization of our land and soil are integral to world trade—as presently constituted to favor the West—but it does very little to enhance human health, psychic wholeness, or spiritual maturation. In the long term, such alienation from the land is likely to wreak havoc on humanity's future. It may well be the most sinister of all the subtle factors that has *Homo sapiens* sliding down an ever more precarious slope to perdition.

A realignment of gigantic proportion awaits us, the dimensions of which are discerned by the naturalist-cum-philosopher David Abram (2010, 77–78):

> It is not only other animals, plants and simpler organisms that have contributed, during the course of evolution, to the unique character of the human creature,

but also the fluid ocean, and the many rocks that
compose the soils, and the way the mountains gather
clouds above the high ridges. These planetary structures are not extrinsic to human life—they are not
arbitrary or random aspects of a world we just happen
to inhabit. Rather they are the constitutive powers that
summoned us into existence, and hence are the secret
allies, the totemic guides, of all our actions. They are as
much within us as they are around us; they compose
the wider deeper life of which our bodies are a part. . . . In a
thoroughly palpable sense we are born of this planet;
our attentive bodies coevolved in rich and intimate
rapport with the other bodily forms—animals, plants,
mountains, rivers—that compose the shifting flesh of
this breathing world.

Every fiber of our being, every motion of our bodies,
and every yearning of the heart arise from in-spirited energy,
embedded in our earth. Our creativity as Earthlings is an inheritance that is earthy and sacred at one and the same time. We
are born out of an eternity that is tangibly near and dear. It is
that ancient generativity shared by insect, plant, and human
alike—and the common denominator uniting and differentiating all three is none other than the Great Spirit, whom our
ancient ancestors long knew and loved.

5

Beneficiaries of an Original Blessing

When the mind can engage reality as a question rather than imposing prefabricated answers on it, then one can participate creatively in evolution.

—Ilia Delio

As a human species we are certainly not getting it right today. To the contrary, we are making life on earth a hell for ourselves and for many other species as well. To the average citizen that is how it has always been, and how often has religion informed us that it will always be that way! Something deep within us militates against the good we desire. St. Paul stated it quite explicitly:

I do not understand what I do. For what I want to do I do not do, but what I hate I do. And if I do what I do not want to do, I agree that the law is good. As it is, it is no longer I myself who do it, but it is sin living in me. For I know that good itself does not dwell in me, that is, in my sinful nature. For I have the desire to do what is good, but I cannot carry it out. For I do not do the good I want to do, but the evil I do not want to

79

do—this I keep on doing. Now if I do what I do not want to do, it is no longer I who do it, but it is sin living in me that does it. (Rom. 7:15–20)

What St. Paul describes as sin is more widely known as *original sin*, an inherited predisposition to do wrong that has always been there and apparently always will be. Original sin has been a hotly debated issue ever since it was first suggested by St. Paul and further elaborated by St. Augustine. As indicated in chapter 1, scholars claim that Augustine misrepresents what Paul actually meant (see Rom. 5:12–21), and most go a great deal further, claiming that there is no basis in Scripture for the doctrine of original sin. In the present work I do not elaborate on these complex theological, scriptural, and historical reasons, which can be referenced elsewhere.

Distorted Symbolism

Instead I want to deepen my argument throughout this book: that humans during our long evolutionary story are fundamentally creative beings, beneficiaries of an *original blessing* and not victims of an original sin. I want to develop this thesis first by revisiting the opening chapters of the book of Genesis and indicate how ancient, rich symbolism became distorted and even demonized with some deeply disturbing results for how human growth and development came to be understood. Let's review a key text:

Then the LORD God said to the woman, "What is this you have done?" And the woman said, "The serpent deceived me, and I ate." The LORD God said to the serpent, "Because you have done this, Cursed are you more than all cattle, And more than every beast of the field; On your belly you will go, And dust you will eat

All the days of your life; And I will put enmity between
you and the woman, and between your seed and her
seed; He shall bruise you on the head, and you shall
bruise him on the heel." (Gen. 3:13–15)

This mythic scriptural conflict between the woman and
the serpent (often called a snake) has been inflated into the primordial curse that humanity must endure until the end of time.
Here the serpent is endowed with Satan-like supremacy, who
lured first the woman and then all humans into an irreversible
state of depravity. Although Christians believe that the death
of Jesus on the cross brings an end to Satan's reign, nonetheless
the sinful contamination symbolized in the serpent beguiles
humans for the rest of their earthly existence.

The demonizing of the serpent provides a classic example
of where humans lost touch with their primordial creativity
as well as their complex unfolding as an evolutionary species.
According to Udo Becker (1994, 343), the symbol of *the serpent* plays an extraordinarily important and extremely diverse
role among several ancient peoples. It is frequently encountered
as a chthonic being, an adversary of mankind, a protector of
sacred precincts or of the underworld, an animal having the
soul of a human, a sexual symbol (masculine because of its
phallic shape, feminine because of its engulfing belly), and a
symbol of a constant power of renewal (because of the shed-
ding of its skin).

In China, the serpent was thought to be connected with
the earth and water, thus perceived to be a *yin* symbol. Indian
mythology has serpents that function as beneficent or maleficent
mediators between gods and humans, known as *nagas,* sometimes (like other serpents in other civilizations) associated with
the rainbow. The kundalini serpent, imagined as being rolled up
at the bottom end of the spine, is regarded as the seat of cosmic
energy, a symbol of life, and a wellspring of human libido.

In the symbolism of the Egyptians, the serpent played an essential and greatly varying role; there were, for example, several serpent goddesses, such as a cobra goddess who presided over the growth of plants. Fate (good or bad) was also sometimes worshiped in the form of a serpent, regarded as a house spirit. The symbol of the *uroboros*, the serpent biting its own tail, first appeared in Egypt.

The worship of the serpent is found in many parts of the Old World, the Americas, and even Australia, where Aboriginal people worship a gigantic python known by various names but typically referred to as the Rainbow Serpent. It was said to have created the landscape, embodied the spirit of fresh water, and punished lawbreakers. The Aborigines in southwest Australia called the mythical serpent the *Waugyl*, while the Warramunga of the east coast worshiped the *Wollunqua*.

In Africa the serpent was occasionally revered in cults as a spirit or Deity. In a cave hidden in the Tsodilo Hills of Botswana, Sheila Coulson, an archaeologist at the University of Oslo in Norway, has made several intriguing discoveries of ancient spirituality-worship, including carvings on a snake-shaped rock along with seventy-thousand-year-old spearheads nearby.

In these varied examples the serpent or snake is, by analogy, symbolic of energy itself—of force pure and simple—hence its ambivalence and multivalences. As we move into the emergence of monotheistic religion about three thousand years ago, the archetypal significance of the serpent/snake is gradually undermined and eroded. Throughout the Hebrew Scriptures, the serpent is depicted as a threatening creature. The Old Testament counts it among the unclean animals; it appears as the idealized image of sin and of Satan, and is the seducer of the first couple in the garden of Eden. Christians fully adopted the negative, sinful portrayal.

Maligning the Tree of Life

Bad as all things have been with the serpent, they get much worse when we come to the tree in the garden (Gen. 2:9; 3:1ff.). It is from the tree in the center of the garden that the poisonous contagion ensues, and the woman will forever remain the pernicious source of that calamity. So, let's begin by asking, where did the writer(s) of Genesis find the myth of the tree?

The world tree is a recurring theme in several ancient religious traditions,[1] frequently represented as a colossal tree that supports the heavens, thereby connecting the heavens, the terrestrial world, and through its roots, the underworld. It may also be strongly connected to the motif of the tree of life. Some scholars suggest that the world tree is programmed into the human mind by evolutionary biology, since we in our primate state lived in trees for several thousand years. The idea of a vast tree as the entirety of the world is thus still implanted in our collective unconscious.

As an enduring religious symbol, the tree denotes fertility, fruitfulness, vitality, protective shade, and an icon standing between the Earth and the upper world. It was a primary symbol of the Great Earth Mother Goddess, and in all probability this is the background against which we need to read Genesis 2–3. First, the garden symbolizes the abundant life of paradise, represented archetypally in the fertile woman who graciously and gratefully receives the fruit from the tree of life.[2] She has been doing this for thousands of years throughout the preagricultural era. She knows intimately and wisely what she is doing. Dysfunctionality takes over when the rational imperial

---

[1] https: en.wikipedia.org/wiki/World_tree.

[2] According to popular belief the fruit of temptation was an apple, but the apple was unknown in the Near East when the Bible was written there.

male wants to grab the fruit and consume it to his own power-laden advantage. In typical patriarchal retort the woman is blamed and scapegoated when in truth it is the male who corrupts the entire plot.

From there on, the rational imperial males misread everything; they are unable to discern according to the wisdom of the Great Spirit. The garden of paradise is now reduced to a once-upon-a-time utopian state in which all was in harmony with God. But according to our long evolutionary narrative, there has never been a time in which we were in complete harmony; nonetheless, while we remained very close to nature, we did essentially get things right. So, the Judeo-Christian myth of an original perfect paradise from which we fell is essentially correct, but it needs to be viewed in evolutionary, not ideological terms. The further suggestion that we will one day return to that idyllic state makes no evolutionary sense.

The plight of the world tree takes on a frightening distortion when the Christian salvation is activated by the crucifixion of Jesus on a dead tree. That outstanding Christian archetypal figure—Jesus as the Christ—represents everything that is wholesome, good, and beautiful about the tree of life in its ancient understanding. What a cruel irony that he was lethally punished for his countercultural vision by being killed on the wood of a dead tree. The very suggestion that salvation—creative life—could emanate from such morbid symbolism vividly portrays how far formal religion can deviate from creative truth.

Pointers to Blessedness

Throughout this book I am running with the suggestion that the current portrayal of the human species as a violent, destructive, and sinfully problematic group is a perception based on the documented anthropology of recent millennia (no more than ten thousand years old) and is not likely to withstand the more sophisticated analysis of earlier times surfacing in contemporary sciences like ethnography, anthropology, paleontology, and ancient history.

Jeremy Rifkin (2009, 18) captivates our enduring dilemma in this cryptic observation:

> Is it possible that human beings are not inherently evil or intrinsically self-interested and materialistic, but are of a very different nature—an empathic one—and that all of the other drives that we have considered to be primary—aggression, violence, selfish behavior, acquisitiveness—are in fact secondary drives that flow from the repression or denial of our most basic instinct?

As a species with an evolutionary story of at least 7 million years, including the proto-human (*Australopithecus*), or 3.3 million years (in the case of our *Homo* designation), we must transcend the narrow, functional, violent portrayal of recent millennia. In all probability, it does not render justice to our larger story; to the contrary, it furnishes a dangerously misleading and distorted picture that fits well with the distorted condition known as original sin.

We also need to outgrow the rather simplistic but widespread rationalization that if we are so dysfunctional today, our ancient ancestors must have been much worse. This is a well-established psycho-cultural ploy known as *projection*. Out of our deluded arrogance we perceive everybody else as inferior to us. The further back the story goes, the more primitive we deem the ancestors to be. We create ancient scapegoats onto whom we project the destructive behaviors in ourselves that we do not like. In so doing, we fail to engage our own dark shadows and begin to reap the results within and without. We never face up to who really has the problem, nor the

frightening prospect that we ourselves need the primary reme-
dial action.

In earlier chapters I outlined some of the indications of
an earlier creative streak that dominated our behavior and
our way of being in the world. I am not trying to claim an
original perfection of any type, simply a conviction that in
previous times we have known and experienced ways of
engaging with life that were far more congruent for us as
Earthlings. Creativity, innovation, exploration, and a sense
of being blessed were our dominant characteristics, resulting
in a convivial relationship with the earth, devoid of much of
the estrangement and alienation so widespread at the present time. In addition to older evidence outlined in previous
chapters, let's now look nearer to our own time for related
evidence indicating how Earthlings exemplified gratitude for
earthly blessings.

In their overview of hunter-gatherer ancestors (dating from
70,000 to 12,000 BCE), anthropologists Flannery and Marcus
(2012, 54) outline the following list of principles that seem to
have undergirded their values and communal behaviors:

1. Generosity is admirable; selfishness is reprehensible.
2. The social relationship created by a gift is more valu-
    able than the gift itself.
3. All gifts should be reciprocated; however, a reasonable
    delay before reciprocating is acceptable.
4. Names are magic and should not be casually assigned.
5. Since all humans are reincarnated, ancestors' names
    should be treated with particular respect.
6. Homicide is unacceptable. A killer's relatives should
    either execute him or pay reparations to the victim's
    family.
7. Do not commit incest; get your spouse from outside
    your immediate kin.

8. In return for a bride, the groom should provide her family with services or gifts.
9. Marriage is a flexible economic partnership; it allows for multiple spouses and variations.

No doubt the contemporary reader will look aghast at number nine above, viewing it as a primitive practice that has been transcended by our more civilized, rational, and moral arrangement of contemporary monogamous marriage. I expect the reader will also be aware of the fact that our world today seems to be reverting to the liberalism and apparent promiscuity of the past. Most people regard this as a seriously disturbing cultural regression. As I suggest later in this chapter, we are dealing with a complex evolutionary imperative that requires a great deal of discerning wisdom.

These guidelines would have been drawn up at a time when none of the contemporary structural guidelines existed. There were no governments as we know them today, no legal systems, and no religious institutions of any type. *Clans*, rather than tribes, seem to have been the prevailing organizational structure. A clan is generally described as a group of people united by actual or perceived kinship and descent. Even if lineage details are unknown, clan members may be organized around a founding ancestor. When this "ancestor" is nonhuman, it is referred to as a totem, which is frequently associated with an animal. Here, I am using the term *clan* to denote a kinship gathering, probably no more than three hundred people, providing one of the earliest forms of social organization known to our species. In all probability the kind of working regulations they drew up would have resembled those outlined above by Flannery and Marcus (2012).

Tribes are a later and more formal development. Retaining the strong kinship ties, they are also identified with a particular geographical area. Whereas the clan may still be quite mobile, the tribe represents a stage in human evolution when we became more sedentary and settled. One also detects in the tribe a movement toward self-sufficiency, whereas the clan belongs more to the peripatetic lifestyle of the hunter-gatherer. In a sense, tribes represent the oldest known form of political organization. Although details are difficult to establish, tribes probably had some differential roles and a structure of authority, most likely with a strong communal undercurrent.

That changes rapidly when we move into the period known as the Agricultural Revolution. *Chiefdoms* come to the fore, with strong linear structures of power from the top down, and increasing levels of hierarchical organization. Tribes also begin to develop rivalries and adopt violence to resolve differences. We are now a short step from the notion of the nation-state.

Meanwhile, the relationship with the land has also changed drastically, from being a universal space for all to wander and savor (the clan) to being a reserved space to be selfishly guarded (the tribe), to being a problematic resource that needed to be controlled and commodified to the advantage of those with power (the chiefdom). With the growing alienation from the land itself, humans also underwent a kind of psychic transformation, from egalitarian, consensual beings to competitive, violent individuals. We forfeited our blessedness for the sake of patriarchal domination.

We see this cultural shift played out in the Jewish Scriptures, as early as the opening chapters of Genesis. All is declared to be good, with humans at home in creation. This overidealized scenario need not be literalized. However, it does highlight a quality of harmony that humans later lost—not because of original sin, I contend, but because of a growing alienation from the land itself, which becomes much more apparent in Genesis 2–3. Humans are no longer at home on the earth, because the aftermath of the Agricultural Revolution has put in place an alienating dynamic.

To address this unfolding cultural and religious dilemma, the Jewish faith formulates the notion of the covenant, a reassurance to the alienated people that they are still loved and cherished by God. At the heart of that covenantal pact is a land flowing with milk and honey, a place of abundance where all the people will truly feel at home. It is a wonderful utopian dream, not without precedent in what went before, but it did not stand a hope of being realized amid the patriarchal turmoil that ensued thereafter.

Indeed, blessedness was the endowment for which humans hungered, because throughout several previous millennia that is what they knew instinctively and intuitively. Now it had been snatched from them, and they longed deeply for its return. Every religion promised an eventual breakthrough, an eschatological utopia, either in this world (Judaism) or in a life beyond (Hinduism, Buddhism, Christianity, Islam). The life beyond this vale of tears was to prove the greatest delusion of all, seriously distracting humans from their empowering relationship with the earth as indigenous Earthlings. It has taken us some ten thousand years to wake up from our patriarchal oppression, and with that awakening we can see the first cracks in the patriarchal edifice. A deeper truth is illuminating our horizon once more.

Evolutionary Promise

As long as we cling to the Judeo-Christian story of origin, we will never make the breakthrough that is necessary for our species survival or for our ongoing growth and development as a responsible evolving group.

This patriarchal/imperial view of creation cannot be reconciled with an evolutionary understanding of life, God, the world, or people. Nor can it be reconciled with the spirituality of the Great Spirit, probably the original creative agent

depicted in the book of Genesis. In seeking to honor and
reclaim the ancient wisdom, and reconstruct it as a spirituality relevant to the twenty-first century, I wish to embrace and
integrate important evolutionary insights of our time.

The Jesuit priest paleontologist Pierre Teilhard de Chardin
(1881–1955) is one of the leading proponents of the evolutionary perspective, bringing us to the threshold of the twenty-first
century, wherein theologians seek a new theological discourse
to rehabilitate Charles Darwin himself (see, e.g., Celia Dean-
Drummond, Elizabeth Johnson, and John F. Haught). Teilhard
himself continues to enjoy a religious and scientific revival
through researchers such as Thomas Berry, Ursula King, and
Ilia Delio (Delio, 2014).

For the purposes of the present work, I do not need to outline the complexities of evolutionary theory but instead focus
on its key meaning, in which it denotes the unceasing process
of change, growth, and development throughout the entire
spectrum of creation. To begin with, I briefly indicate what I
mean by an *evolutionary perspective*, highlighting the following characteristics that are central to the sense of creativity and
blessedness I am seeking to reclaim in the present work.

1. *Aliveness.* Over the past twenty years our understanding of aliveness has changed dramatically. The propensity for
aliveness is no longer reserved to the human, deemed to be
superior to all other life forms. On the contrary, we know that
everything that constitutes our embodiment as Earthlings is
given to us from Earth itself, as a living organism, itself energized from the larger cosmic web of life. In scriptural terms
the catalyst for this aliveness is the creative energy described
as *Memra/Dabar* (more in chapter 9 below), and theologically
this translates into the Holy Spirit that enlivens all that exists
(Boff 2015; Haughey 2015). In this context, aliveness is a primary creative feature of every life form, organic and nonor-
ganic alike. Consequently, our experience of human aliveness is

an endowment derived from the cosmic web, and neither alien nor superior to everything else that exists. Moreover, that aliveness is the springboard for all creativity, human and nonhuman alike. It is also the wellspring of the blessedness we know when we remain close to the living earth itself.

2. *Emergence.* The all-embracing sense of aliveness unfolds along an evolutionary trajectory that transcends simple cause-and-effect, with a sense of direction that is open and unpredictable, always evolving into greater complexity (for further elaboration, see Delio 2015; Stewart 2000). This growth into greater complexity is the evolutionary equivalent of the creative imperative, which never ceases to unfold and complexify. In this case, nothing in creation stands still or remains static. Humans are evolutionary processes rather than creatures trying to manage and control creation's explosive fertility. This emergent dynamic is consistently undermined by our human urge to dominate and control. Our patriarchal resistance to organic growth and its accompanying cultural diversity will not halt evolution's forward movement; it will simply add additional pain and misery to our human predicament—unless and until we reawaken to our deeper meaning as evolutionary beings.

3. *Paradox.* Despite this creative compelling urge, chance and necessity continue to inform all that grows and unfolds. Nothing is definitively guaranteed, yet everything is endowed with a creative potential that rational humans cannot fully comprehend. What's more, creation's evolutionary unfolding is endowed with the paradoxical interplay of creation-cum-destruction, an unceasing cyclic rhythm of birth-death-rebirth. Major religions tend to dismiss this paradox as a fundamental flaw requiring divine salvific intervention, particularly through the death and resurrection of the historical Jesus. A deeper appreciation of this enduring paradox alters significantly our understanding of suffering in the world and evokes a whole

new collaborative response, challenging humans themselves to engage proactively with the destructive elements of life instead of waiting for some divine rescuer to sort it all out on our behalf. Currently we meet suffering with desperation and often with a cold sense of resignation. Evolution illuminates another path, imbued with a paradoxical wisdom inscribed throughout the creative universe itself.

4. *Lateral thinking.* Much of Christian theology and the ensuing spirituality is defined and described in terms of classical Greek metaphysics, rational thought, and logical argument (already highlighted in previous chapters). It is a linear, sequential process favored by dominant males seeking control and mastery through rational discourse. It is a strategy alien to evolutionary unfolding, lacking in the creativity, imagination, and intuition necessary to apprehend the complexities of this age and every other. Beyond the traditional affiliation with scholastic philosophy, both theology and spirituality must now embrace a multidisciplinary dynamic to engage the lateral consciousness of the twenty-first century and push humanity itself toward expanded horizons of comprehension, reflection, and discernment.

5. *Consciousness.* The metaphysical worldview also favored the philosophy of divide and conquer, thus segmenting wisdom and knowledge into binary opposites (dualisms) and uniform categories, alien to the multidisciplinary and transdisciplinary philosophy of our age. According to this latter view, a multidisciplinary perspective is necessary to comprehend the complex and creative nature of all living reality. Consequently, Scripture scholars, in particular, are increasingly adopting a multidisciplinary orientation in their research and discernment, embracing a range of social sciences as well as the wisdom of ancient history and the corroborative evidence of archaeological discoveries. Contrary to the fear of several fundamentalists, such a broad interdisciplinary base—a new quality of

consciousness—does not diminish the truth of faith, but for a growing body of adult faith-seekers enriches and deepens their spirituality.

6. *Spirituality.* All over the contemporary world, mainline religion is in recession (with the possible exception of Islam), yielding pride of place either to more amorphous spiritual offshoots or to violent ideologies that will eventually destroy the very religion they seek to safeguard and promote. Nearly all formal religious traditions embody imperial sentiment, a derogatory view of creation, and a distinctly male, patriarchal bias. An alternative spiritual hunger has surfaced many times in the history of the great religions, and frequently has been suppressed; it sometimes morphs into a phenomenon known as *mysticism*, which has enjoyed a distinctive revival in recent decades (see Johnson & Ord 2012). And as already indicated, the empowering presence of God, under the rubric of the Great Spirit, takes on an unprecedented significance for our time.

7. *Cooperation.* From a human perspective, evolution is not solely dependent on the survival of the fittest, but rather on the triumph of cooperation. For John Stewart, cooperation is evolution's arrow: "Cooperators will inherit the earth, and eventually the universe" (2000, 8). However, it has to be a quality of cooperation that can embrace and integrate legitimate self-interest. This is the kind of integration that wise elders desire, and it is remarkably similar to the supreme goal of both Judaism and Christianity: Love God! And to do that, one has to love the neighbor, which is only genuinely possible when we learn to love ourselves (cf. Lev. 19:18; Mark 12:29–30). Genuine self-interest is not contrary to faith in God or to faith in evolution; it is the prerequisite for both.

Our evolutionary propensities mark a seismic shift from a worldview in which we were "captivated by the spell of solidity, the fallacy of fixity, the illusion of immobility, the semblance of stasis, but the evolution revolution is starting to break that spell. We are realizing that we are, in fact, not standing on solid ground. But neither are we adrift in a meaningless universe. . . . We are part and parcel of a vast process of becoming" (Phipps 2012, 26). Phipps (32) goes on to identify three characteristics common to evolutionary thinkers and to the wise elders of the twenty-first century:

- Evolutionary thinkers are cross-disciplinary generalists.
- Evolutionary thinkers develop the capacity to cognize the vast timescales of our evolutionary history.
- Evolutionary thinkers embody a new spirit of optimism.

This spirit of optimism is one important dimension of the spiritual convergence characterizing our time. Scientists are sometimes ahead of religionists in viewing a spiritual way forward: "In recent years there has been a resurgence of interest in the connections that might serve to reunify the scientific world-view with the religious instinct. Much of the discussion is tentative, and the difficulties in finding an accommodation remain daunting, but it is more than worth the effort. In my opinion, it will be our lifeline" (Conway Morris 2003, 328).

Our age is characterized by a deepening awareness of how central evolutionary thinking has become to how we view our world. Above and beyond the complex ideas of the neo-Darwinian synthesis, we can name three processes that characterize evolutionary growth at every level, from the bacterial to the cosmic domains:

1. Everything within and around us *grows*; that seems an indisputable fact of the natural and human worlds.

2. We perceive *change* all around us, which involves decline and death. Such disintegration is not an evil, nor is it the consequence of sin (see Rom. 6:23), but a God-given dimension impacting the growth and development of everything in creation.

3. Clearly evolution builds on the successes of the past, but evolution is also indebted to a *generic lure from the future.* This insight, originally formulated by the philosopher Karl Popper, has been articulated afresh by the contemporary theologian John F. Haught (2010; 2015). For Haught, evolution is not merely about solidifying what has served us well in the past, but rather is propelled by a powerful lure from the future: "Evolution, viewed theologically, means that creation is still happening and that God is creating and saving the world not *a retro*, that is, by pushing it forward out of the past, but *ab ante*, by calling it from up ahead" (2015, 52). Theologically, I understand the lure of the future to be the fruit and wisdom of the Holy Spirit.

Holding On to Hope

Throughout this chapter I have reviewed our human evolutionary story as a narrative marked with innumerable blessings. Creativity abounds, if only we could see. To transcend our cultural blindness, reinforced by so many ideologies—religious and otherwise—we need to reclaim afresh two enduring evolutionary imperatives:

- We are Earthlings, and our earth-identity is foundational to our propensity for growth and meaning.
- That same growth is fueled by an evolutionary imperative in which nothing stands still, and in which everything complexifies through a spiritual readiness to flow where evolution leads us.

Faced with such formidable challenges, we can easily capitulate to despair and helplessness, particularly as our education and faith development have failed to prepare us for this evolutionary hour. Whether we can keep hope alive very much depends on how we welcome and embrace this evolutionary challenge.

I continue to hold on to hope despite the widespread cynicism and pessimism of our times, and therefore I continue to offer the possibility of optimistic outcomes. Faced with the positive overview of the present chapter, the reader cannot be blamed for reacting with skepticism and even incredulity. The world we inhabit today is so fractured and demented with meaningless pain, anguish, and suffering, it is indeed enormously difficult to see any empowering creativity at work.

Paradoxically, it is when we humans are faced with the dark abyss that we rise to challenges that seem insurmountable at other times. It is precisely when we thought that all hope had faded that God or the universe (perhaps both) reminds us that we are indeed creatures endowed with a quality of creativity that cannot be conquered. How I wish we could hold on to that transformative hope!

Our inherited Christian story must carry at least some of the blame for the disconnectedness that undermines hope and optimism, often focusing on sin and depravity instead of calling us to the grandeur of who and what we are destined to become as evolutionary Earthlings. Yet even within Christianity itself lies a creative and hope-filled strand, the resilience of life that endures even amid the dark clouds of hopelessness and despair. We seek to plumb those paradoxical depths in the next chapter.

6

Who Put God on Another-World Throne?

Augustus introduced the imperial cult to Rome itself. . .
. In effect, he remodeled the ancient practice of ancestral
worship into the worship of himself and his family rather
as Confucianism had molded the age-old ancestor wor-
ship of China into a doctrine of devotion to the Emperor.

—Selina O'Grady

Contrary to all the great religions, I want to run with the controversial notion that the oldest religion known to our species is something akin to the indigenous/tribal notion of the
Great Spirit. This transcendent force that energizes life, for
aeons beyond human measuring, is a life force of pure creative energy. It transcends all material, physical, embodied, and
human form, yet reveals itself through embodied structure,
where the emphasis is primarily on blessed potential and not
on fundamental flaw. The oldest and most enduring manifestation of the Great Spirit is the open-ended quantum universe,
without beginning or end. The Great Spirit continues to cocre-
ate through stars, galaxies, planets, bacteria, plants, fishes, and
animals, and in more recent millennia, through humans.

In terms of the Spirit's creative prerogative, all the above articulations are revelatory, sacred, and unique. None can claim superiority to any other. All are necessary to illustrate and illuminate the mystery to which we all belong and without which our existence is not even possible. Central to that mystery is a capacity for creativity common to Gods and humans alike.

Like all the other articulations, humans also are unique. We do seem to be endowed with the most sophisticated levels of self-reflexive consciousness—the ability to think about the fact that we can think—above and beyond any other organic creature. That is our uniqueness, the special endowment we have chosen to use to our selfish advantage over everything else in creation. To the degree that we have adapted such a deviation, we are remarkable for our deviancy as much as for our uniqueness. Some people speculate that the dinosaurs attempted similar superiority over every other life form, which, with hindsight, seems to have been the cause of their downfall and their eventual extinction.[1]

When, why, and how did humans betray and deviate from the inclusive organic web of cosmic and planetary coexistence? That is the dilemma I am attempting to resolve in the present chapter. First I examine some of our inherited notions of God and divine agency at work in our world. Contrary to the notion of the Great Spirit (outlined above), the God-concept in most of the currently extant world religions is that of a patriarchal, imperial figurehead employing various levels of redemptive violence, and this sanctioned violence is at the root

---

[1] "Going the way of the dinosaurs" usually denotes species extinction, which is commonly postulated on the destructive impact of a meteorite or some other extraterrestrial force. This leading theory is an assumption rather than a proven fact, and largely based on American/European scholarship. There are a range of other possibilities—reviewed by Parsons (2004)—including that of self-destruction, due to their negative powerful impact on other life forms.

of many of the major problems facing humanity today. In so many political and economic contexts, as well as social and religious ones, this inherited religious ideology exerts an influence far beyond its usefulness. In several cases, it is even a deviation from the deeper meaning of the religions themselves.

The Notion of God

Across the world's main religions, one encounters diverse views on the meaning of God and God's influence on human affairs. The great religions of the East, frequently dismissed as paganism, embody creative dimensions far in excess of the dominant monotheistic faiths of the West. By the same token, the great Eastern religions are not as explicitly guilt-focused as are Judaism, Christianity, and Islam. Instead the great Eastern religions uphold and foster an understanding of life—human and other—embracing a foundational sense of paradox (outlined in chapter 5 above) rather than the Western (Hellenistic) tendency toward dualistic splitting of good vs. evil, the sacred vs. the mundane, and so on. I suggest that the empowering mystery that we normally describe as God is much more transparent in the Eastern faith systems than in the monotheistic religions, which are largely concerned with a transcendent patriarchal figurehead of unquestioned power and domination.

First I offer the reader a brief overview of the empowering sense of mystery exhibited by the great Eastern religions. *Jainism* does not support belief in a creator God. According to Jain doctrine, the universe and its constituents—soul, matter, space, time, and principles of motion—have always existed. All the constituents and actions are governed by universal natural laws. It is not possible to create matter out of nothing, and hence the sum total of matter in the universe remains the same (similar to the law of conservation of mass). Jain texts claim that the universe consists of *Jiva* (life force or souls) and

Ajiva (lifeless objects). Similarly, the soul of each living being is unique and uncreated and has existed from time immemorial. Parallels with the notion of the Great Spirit are readily discernible.

Moral rewards and sufferings are not the work of a divine being, but a result of an innate moral order in the cosmos—a self-regulating mechanism whereby individuals reap the fruits of their own actions, similar to the notion of karma in Hinduism and Buddhism. The individual believer is challenged to live nonviolently, subduing unruly passions and desires, in order to live more benevolently with the natural rhythms of creation. Jainism asserts that a religious and virtuous life is possible without the idea of a creator God.

In *Hinduism*, the concept of God spans conceptions from absolute monism to henotheism, monotheism, and polytheism. In the Advaita Vedanta school of Hindu philosophy the notion of *Brahman* (the highest Universal Principle) is akin to that of God, except that unlike most other philosophies, Advaita likens Brahman to Atman (the true Self of an individual). This tendency to blur the distinctions between the sacredness of God and the sacred in everything else results in the notion of the numerous *devas*. *Deva* may be roughly translated into English as Deity, demigod, or angel, and can describe any celestial being or thing that carries sacred significance.

The word "Brahman" is derived from the verb *brh* (Sanskrit: to grow), and denotes greatness and infinity. While Brahman tends to be described as eternal, unchanging, infinite, immanent, and transcendent reality, the more foundational meaning is that of the Divine Ground of all matter, energy, time, space, being, and everything beyond in this universe. The nature of Brahman is described as transpersonal, personal, and impersonal by different philosophical schools. Once again, I draw the reader's attention to possible parallels with the notion of the Great Spirit.

The Trinitarian aspect of Hinduism seems more foundational than the divine imperial status of any one of its individual deities. Derived from Sanskrit, the Hindu *Trimūrti* describes the Hindu trinity with the triple cosmic functions of creation, maintenance, and destruction. The three functions tend to be associated with Brahman, the creator; Vishnu, the preserver; and Shiva, the destroyer/regenerator. The collaboration of the three depicts a more creative meaning for the divine interaction with all creation.

Buddhism tends to be described as a nontheistic religion; belief in a divine Deity is generally considered not to be an integral dimension. However, some teachers instruct students beginning Buddhist meditation that the notion of divinity is not incompatible with Buddhism, but dogmatic beliefs in a supreme personal creator are considered a hindrance to the attainment of nirvana (liberation), the highest goal of Buddhist practice. In Buddhism, the sole aim of the spiritual practice is the complete alleviation of suffering (*dukka*), and the achievement of harmonious coexistence with everything in life.

Despite its apparent nontheism, Buddhists consider veneration of the Noble Ones as being important to their belief system, although the two main schools of Buddhism differ in their interpretation. While Theravada Buddhists view the Buddha as a human being who attained nirvana or arahanthood through human efforts, Mahayana Buddhists consider him an embodiment of the cosmic *dharmakaya* (a notion of transcendent divinity), who was born for the benefit of others and not merely a human being. In addition, some Mahayana Buddhists worship their chief Bodhisattva, a unique embodiment of the divine in human form.

Despite these theoretical (theological) considerations that often preoccupy scholars, for Buddhists generally it is the focus on meditation and mindfulness that is viewed as of primary practical value. Buddhism claims that, through faithful practice

of mindfulness, humans can exercise an intelligent relationship with creation, such that the realization of an underlying
empowering wisdom (what other religions call *God*) comes to
greater fruition in the world.

Contrary to the more esoteric nature of the great Eastern religions, the Western perspective is distinctly imperial and
anthropomorphic in nature. Depicting God as *a great ruling
king* is a central feature, often understated because of the preoccupation to uphold the primacy of monotheism as a more
authentic understanding of God and of how the divine governance is exercised in the world.

The Option for Monotheism

In religious scholarship, especially in the West, the evolution
of monotheism is widely considered to be a development of
maturity leading to deeper truth. Monotheism promotes the
idea that God should be regarded as a unified wholeness. This
can translate into an understanding of God as solely one—
person or entity—as in the Muslim faith, or as a combination
of descending expressions all accountable to one source (also
called *henotheism*). In the case of Christianity, despite its belief
in three "persons" named Father, Son, and Holy Spirit, there
has always been a clear understanding that the diversity of the
three is unambiguously subservient to the one overriding reality that Christians call *God*.

The rise of monotheistic religion is usually attributed to
the Egyptian pharaoh Akhenaton in the fourteenth century
BCE. Although the evidence is circumstantial, it seems that
Moses, who lived around that time, assimilated this concept
of one God, taking it into the desert with him. Thus the Jewish
religion—and its key notion of the "chosen people"—developed along monotheistic lines, as did Christianity and Islam
in later times.

To many contemporary peoples, the notion of God favoring one nation or people above all others sounds ideological, preposterous, and reminiscent of religion's worst forms of oppression. Pressing the rhetoric into an inclusive claim is also difficult, as Frank Spina sought to do in the following quote:

> God did not choose Israel in order to preserve Israelites while condemning all others. That is not the way either election or exclusion works in the Old Testament. Israel was not chosen in order to keep everyone else out of God's fold; Israel was chosen to make it possible for everyone else eventually to be included. It would be a mistake to construe Israel's exclusive election as a function of its superiority. On the contrary, Israel's exclusive status is completely a function of what might be called God's exclusive status. (2006, 6)

Jews and Christians naively assume that the notion of the chosen people is a construct of great age and deep wisdom when in fact it is a very recent development in the evolution of religious consciousness. Moreover, scholars following the line of Jon Assmann (2010, 31) claim that the juxtaposition of monotheism and polytheism is a much later development, arising from the theological debates of the seventeenth and eighteenth centuries. For some, the opposite of monotheism is not polytheism (worshiping many Gods) but the worship of false idols, thus failing to honor the one true God, the origin of unifying truth. The worship of false idols leads to false truths, while—according to monotheistic religion—allegiance to the one God provides a more reliable pathway to unifying truth.

Jon Assmann (2010) suggests that the real opposite of monotheism is not polytheism but *cosmotheism*, the religion of an immanent God, which polytheistic belief systems strive to uphold by proposing various expressions of the divine in the divergent aspects of the created world. For Assmann, therefore,

> The divine cannot be divorced from the world. Mono-theism, however, sets out to do just that. The divine is emancipated from its symbiotic attachment to the cosmos, society, and fate, and turns to face the world as a sovereign power. In the same stroke humanity is likewise emancipated from its symbiotic relationship with the world, and develops in partnership with the one God. (2010, 41)

The monotheistic Deity thus reinforces the long history of patriarchal domination in a belief system that claims there can only be one unambiguous source for divine and earthly power. Effectively this translates into a system that disempowers and disenfranchises not only humans but the living Earth itself and the divine presence immanent in the whole creation. To this extent, monotheism resembles a political ideology rather than a religious belief, one that reinforces patriarchal power and domination and correspondingly undermines the empowering creativity being explored in the present work.

In fact, that superior divine status that belongs explicitly to the monotheistic faiths of Judaism, Christianity, and Islam seems to have influenced the popular understanding of the divine in all the great religions. All over the modern world, we project onto God an ambivalent hunger around power and control. Three key words come to the fore:

1. *Omnipotent.* God is postulated to be all powerful and therefore a resource for humans who feel a sense of powerless-ness. In preagricultural times, there is little evidence to show that humans suffered from such powerlessness. The convivial relation-ship with the earth enabled Earthlings to live meaningfully with paradox and even with contradiction. Every life dilemma did not

have to be resolved, but instead just lived with or lived through. It is after humans become disconnected from the land that we feel the need for an external "divine" source to sort out everything for us. And in our desperation we are not satisfied with a helper or befriending Deity. No, he must be all powerful—in the hope that humans themselves can outwit the problematic earth, *which had become increasingly strange to the Earthlings.*

2. *Omniscient.* Since everything has now become uncertain and unreliable in the postagricultural dispensation, Earthlings need a God-figure who knows it all and whose wisdom hopefully can empower them to become more skilled and clever in their attempts to conquer and control the wayward creation. The wisdom arising from our convivial relationship with creation was no longer satisfactory for our new anthro pocentric urge to become a dominant species over all else in creation. The omniscient Deity arose from an actual projection of our newly acquired helplessness, which—itself—arose from our disconnection from the sustaining web of life.

3. *Omnipresent.* For much of the Paleolithic epoch—2.6 mya until about twelve thousand 12,000 years ago—humans befriended God as the Great Earth Mother, whose presence among us was believed to be one with the earth itself. The notion of an absent God made no experiential sense. Now in postagricultural times God has been projected above the sky. The mighty divine ruler might be all-powerful and all-knowing, but because he is thought to belong primarily to the heavenly realm, then we detect a lack of spiritual intimacy, which we seek to resolve by declaring God to be omnipresent, a rather strange resolution for cosmic homelessness. The omnipresence is also closely aligned with the projection of being all-powerful; they fit hand in glove.

These three characteristics became the foundational philosophical tenets upon which we have constructed our theology of God. My contention in this chapter is that this all-powerful theodicy misrepresents the creativity of God and undermines our God-given resourcefulness to respond as creative creatures.

Toward a New Reign of God

All of this brings me to a highly contentious claim—namely, that the promulgation of "the kingdom of God" (the reign of God) in the Christian Gospels consciously seeks to undo the inherited patriarchal imperial monopoly and reclaim once more the foundational spiritual creativity long known to the human species. My intention is not to set Judaism and Christianity on an adversarial course, with Christianity emerging as the more authentic expression. Rather I am embracing and endorsing a thesis I first came across in the work of the American scholar Thomas Sheehan, who claims that in the promulgation of the kingdom of God Jesus was seeking the end to all formal religion in favor of a more dynamic and empowering spirituality. Thus, Sheehan writes,

> Jesus did not undertake his prophetic mission in order to bring people more religion (surely there was enough available already), or a different religion (Judaism was quite adequate, as religions go), or the true and perfect religion (which would be a contradiction in terms), nor was his goal to reform the religion into which he was born. Rather, Jesus preached the end of religion and the beginning of what religion is supposed to be about: God's presence among men and women. . . . His proclamation marked the end of religion and religion's God. (1986, 222, 61; also 68, 173)

In previous works (O'Murchu 2011; 2014a) I have attempted a synthesis of how contemporary Scripture scholars and theologians are developing this highly complex creative notion of the kingdom of God. It is very much a work in progress, with a gathering momentum that the challenge in the Sermon in the Mount to seek *first* the kingdom of God (Matt. 6:33) has not been honored in the history of Christendom, and has yet to become an integral dimension of our leading ecclesiologies. Ever since the time of the Roman emperor Constantine, Christianity has adopted an imperial understanding of God and Jesus, a mode of divine rulership modeled on the all-powerful earthly king, itself derived from the kinglike God governing from beyond the sky.

Throughout the latter half of the twentieth century, Scripture scholars and theologians broke through the imperial consciousness that had controlled thinking minds for much of Christendom and began to question a great deal of inherited biblical wisdom. In the case of Jesus, theologians and Scripture scholars began to clear away the clutter of imposed imperial conditioning, culminating in a critical reassessment of one central feature—rendered in the Gospels as the kingdom of God.

The word *kingdom* denotes kingship, royal privilege, and royal power. For much of the Christian era Jesus was regarded and worshiped as a king, with all the pomp and glory of an earthly monarch—and a great deal more. Jesus was the true king, the perfect earthly icon of the supreme reigning God above the skies.

It took Christians almost two thousand years to realize that the notion of the kingdom of God was not in fact an endorsement of everything that kingship represented. To the contrary, it was a phrase with a complex meaning, infused with ambiguity and paradox. Gradually scholars began to realize that Jesus used the phrase in a highly equivocal and provocative manner. Jesus *challenged* kingship and all its inherent values; more shocking still, he denounced it to the point of ridicule and insignificance. As one scholar puts it, Jesus was laying the foundations for "an upside-down Kingdom" (Kraybill 1990).

There was more to be unearthed, and this aspect is still under scholarly scrutiny: Jesus spoke in Aramaic, not in the language of the Gospels, namely Greek. All the parables, the Sermon on the Mount, and several of the witty, pithy sayings attributed to Jesus in the Gospels were originally spoken in Aramaic. The English words "kingdom of God" are a direct translation from the Greek: *baslileia tou theou*. Aramaic renders a somewhat different construct based on much more nuanced meanings.

Already in the 1960s, Sverre Aalen (1962) claimed that whereas the kingly language of Judaism was describing a theophanic appearance of God's rule (in chronological terms), Jesus tends to use spatial metaphors with particular focus on *the household* and the collaborative interdependence entailed in such convivial fellowship. Renaming the kingdom of God therefore as "God's household" is a currently popular approach (see Crosby 2012). Another suggested rendering, which I follow throughout the rest of this book, is that of the *Companionship of Empowerment* (see more in Crossan 1991, 421–22; 1997, 42; 1998, 337). Jesus was trying to convey this connotation of empowerment, and quite likely this is the nuanced meaning that the hearers would have appropriated. As a translation of the Aramaic, the phrase "kingdom of God" is not just an inadequate rendering. It may actually be a false representation of what Jesus intended.

From Power to Empowerment

The Aramaic word for "kingdom" is *malkuta*, formed around the root *kut*, which carries strong connotations of empowerment: *power with* rather than *power over*. Empowerment can be facilitated by a benign patriarchal ruler: empower-

ment from the top down. But it seems that even this media-
tion of empowerment was not acceptable to Jesus. It had to
be empowerment *through the process of mutuality*—particularly through the structure of the household, in both its local
and global significance. The pyramid had to become a circle.
Gospel empowerment was to be circular, mutual, interactive,
mobilizing diverse gifts, interpersonal, and lateral. It was not
to be linear in any sense—hence the significance of the word:
companionship.

A radical new prophetic endeavor was coming into being.
Apparently, the disempowered masses embraced it. The powers
that be at the time became more and more threatened. They
scapegoated the empowerer. And they *crucified* him—a form
of Roman execution not for common criminals, or even outrageous ones, but for *subversives* who were perceived as posing
a serious threat to the establishment.

It has taken Christianity two thousand years to catch up
with Jesus as the primary disciple of the Companionship of
Empowerment. The early church, it seems, grasped the vision,
but how coherently and succinctly we will probably never fully
know. The primordial dream might have flourished had not
Constantine usurped and compromised the vision to enhance
and promote his own hunger for power. He legalized Christianity (following the wishes of his predecessor, Gelarius), pav-
ing the way for it to become the official religion of the Roman
Empire toward the end of the fourth century: the greatest
betrayal Christianity has ever known.

By the time of Constantine's death in 337 CE, Christianity
had become an ideology of power. The hierarchy of the day
was ebullient, while others felt that the integrity of the Jesus
vision had been compromised beyond recognition. In protest
they fled to the desert, seeking to recapture in the nascent
monastic movement something of the original purity of their
faith. Meanwhile, Jesus himself had been exalted both

politically and doctrinally, and the Christian creed encapsu-
lated the honorific status for several centuries afterward.

Thanks to the more penetrating and discerning scholarship of the twentieth and twenty-first centuries, we are striving
to reclaim the more authentic Christ-figure of Gospel lore.[2]
This task will never be complete, and we are learning to live
with historical gaps and a range of unanswered questions. In a
sense, the scholarly endeavor is more successful at identifying
the cultural and religious baggage that needs to be discarded
than at portraying an authentic Jesus story that will honor the
past and inspire us for the future. Despite such limitations,
the ring of truth is more transparent and appealing to vast
numbers of more adult Christians today; in several cases—perhaps not surprisingly—such fresh insights are denounced and
rejected by church authorities.

Throughout the remainder of this book I adopt the notion
of the Companionship of Empowerment as what I consider to
be a more faithful rendering of the Gospel vision and therefore
the central focus for living the Christian faith in this age and
every other. In the onerous task of trying to speak truth to
power, we need to expose the cult of power that prevailed at
the time of Jesus, unmask its power-driven controlling dynam-

---

[2] For much of Christian history, we upheld a rather uniform view of
Jesus as the unique divine revelation of the ruling God. In the nineteenth
century, scholars initiated the search for the historical Jesus, a process that
continues to our time, with a plethora of interpretations as illustrated in
the major studies of scholars such as John P. Meier, N. T. Wright, James G.
Dunn, and others (see the valuable overviews in Boulton 2008; Schweitzer
2010). Additionally, I suggest that the postcolonial perspective provides
a more penetrating and timely analysis (see my summary in O'Murchu
2014a). The distinction between the Jesus of history and the Christ of faith
no longer provides clarity for the contemporary believer. How to integrate
wisdom from both sources continues to be a perennial challenge yielding
more diverse but inspiring outcomes—as illustrated in Patterson (2014)
and Spong (2016).

ics, and discern what seems to be of primary significance for Jesus then and now.

Viewing the resurrection as a transformative experience of the early witnesses also is more congruent and respectful of the empowering subversive One who was snatched away by an untimely death. The whole life of Jesus—and the premature death—had one central goal: the Companionship of Empowerment. While Christendom has continued to proclaim Jesus as an archetypal hero, particularly in his death and resurrection, we need to reclaim the subverted communal context of the new companionship. Here we focus primarily on the life of Jesus and not on his salvific death. And then the resurrection of Jesus needs to be reconceptualized in its relation to Jesus's life and not just as a consequence of his death.

There is a postcolonial logic in viewing the resurrection as an empowering set of visions that reenergized the petrified witnesses and helped to regroup them into a companionship that would embark on the rising of a new covenantal people. Instead of focusing on what happened to Jesus in terms of resurrection, often elaborated in terms of a resuscitated divine hero, an empowering creative faith has much more to gain by focusing on the ensuing transformation of the early followers (particularly the women), inspired and empowered by the Christ who "arose" within and among them.

The resurrection narrative marks the end of imperial kingship, as the first witnesses are launched on an empowering mission to Galilee (Matt. 28:7)—where Jesus first proclaimed the new reign of God. In the disciples' transformative resurrection experience, *We got rid of the imperial king!* The male evangelists desperately tried to cling on to the imperial power and glory—as did several subsequent generations of church leaders—but those who carried resurrection hope to Galilee and beyond were endowed with a different, nonimperial, nonviolent dream.

All of this leaves the Christian faith today with an almost

insurmountable problem: *we have obliterated the original witnesses.* The first postresurrection disciples were not the Twelve, nor the Seventy-Two, but a group of women (which probably did include men) inspired and led by Mary Magdalene. That group kept alive the fire for empowerment; they became the first champions of the new companionship. Long before the Twelve returned for Pentecost—if they ever did—the ecclesial empowering community had already been established—not along imperial lines but as a subversive, egalitarian, empowering community as initially inspired by the living witness of the historical Jesus.

As long as the Christian church(es) continue to cling to imperialism and the cult of kingship, they will remain not merely a church in crisis but an idolatrous fabrication, built on false foundations. Jesus never adopted kingship; he forthrightly denounced it in all its vestiges. The risen Christ, embodied in the first disciples (primarily Mary Magdalene and her companions), transcended the colonial residue. The nonimperial foundations were firmly established, and sooner or later the Christian faith community must come to terms with that subversive fact.

Scripture scholar Elisabeth Schüssler Fiorenza threw down the gauntlet in 1983 with the publication of her foundational work *In Memory of Her.* She built on the groundwork of earlier decades and was followed by a plethora of professional studies on the role of women in the Gospels and in early Christian times (see Kramer & d'Angelo 1999; Bauckham 2002; Cooper 2013). The truth too long subverted is beginning to haunt the Christian community. It is only a matter of time until we reach the postcolonial critical mass, and then the radiant truth of the gospel will illuminate what we have for too long preached but not practiced: Seek *first* the new reign of God and its justice . . . and all the rest will fall into place (Matt. 6:33).

On June 2, 1953, Elizabeth was crowned Queen of England. The pompous ceremony included an anointing of hands and head, understood to be a divine unction conferring God-like power. In the same ceremony she was also conferred with the status of being priest, prophet, and king, an attribution to Jesus never explicitly made in Scripture but declared in the *Catechism of the Catholic Church* (nos. 897–913). Invoked in this attribution is "the divine right of kings" to bolster and boost secular power.

My concern, however, is not the secular domain but the several ways in which imperialism has penetrated the very core of our faith, leaving us with a legacy that glorifies the few and disenfranchises the masses. It dealt a severe blow to the foundational creativity of the Christian faith. It is never what God or Jesus intended for followers of the gospel.

7

Politics That Empower

*During periods of discontinuous, abrupt change, the
essence of adaptation involves a keen sensitivity to what
should be abandoned—not what should be changed or
introduced. A willingness to depart from the familiar
has distinct survival value.*

—Peter Drucker

Humans are creative by nature, a status that for the religionist
at least may be considered an outrageous and controversial
claim of this book. It is a prehistoric creativity deeply rooted
in our ancient origins and throughout our long evolutionary
story. It also plumbs subliminal depths to which rational reason and academic learning have only limited access. Human
creativity belongs to the realm of the archetypal.

Archetypal wisdom comes to the surface in the realm of
the imagination, in dreams and fantasies, disdainful to our
rational culture. Amid the ensuing intolerance, discernment of
deeper meaning is likely to be sparse and intermittent. Archetypal upsurges follow few if any rational rules. It is the kind
of wisdom that hits us in the face when we least expect it,

although with hindsight we can detect cultural awakenings that give it a measure of contextual meaning and enduring authenticity.

One such moment was in May 1994 when the recently liberated Nelson Mandela (d. 2013) gave his presidential address to the newly formed South African Parliament. The excitement was tangible and overloaded with hope and subtle meaning. The two inaugural addresses (May 9 and 10) are available online. Neither of them contain the words frequently attributed to Mandela, archetypal words that certainly captivated the sheer mystique of the moment, but originating elsewhere. I adopt the inspirational quote, actually composed by Marianne Williamson, popular American author and spiritual guide:

> Our deepest fear is not that we are inadequate. Our deepest fear is that we are powerful beyond measure. It is our light, not our darkness that most frightens us. We ask ourselves, who am I to be brilliant, gorgeous, talented, and fabulous? Actually, who are you not to be? You are a child of God. Your playing small does not serve the world. There is nothing enlightened about shrinking so that other people will not feel insecure around you. We are all meant to shine, as children do. We were born to make manifest the glory of God that is within us. It is not just in some of us; it is in everyone and as we let our own light shine, we unconsciously give others permission to do the same. As we are liberated from our own fear, our presence automatically liberates others. (Williamson 1992, 190–91)

Although not spoken by Mandela himself nor quoted in his inaugural speeches, the words not only capture Mandela's visionary optimism and prophetic stature but illuminate in sharp relief the political revolution he deeply desired and worked so hard to bring about. In the present chapter I want to use this inspiring passage to critique the debilitating politics of our time, their extensive undermining of human creativity, and the alternative political strategies so urgently needed if we are to recapture and rehabilitate the true spirit of human creativity.

Our Political Dysfunctionality

Foundational to our current social organization and systemic structure is that we begin with the false premise that *we are a flawed species*! Take, for instance, the politics that underpin our economics. Politics throughout most of the modern world operates on the basis of management and control. Although empowerment is the oft-stated goal, only the wealthy and powerful enjoy the benefits. Well over half the human race are mere pundits of a system that lures peoples into cultural collusions that pacify but neither empower nor enrich.

Financially, virtually all major governments follow the same economic ideology: the goods of creation are *scarce*; to avail of the scarce goods we need a competitive system, and capitalism has proved to be the best strategy we have thus far evolved. It sounds rational and reasonable, but it is a delusory system that leads to widespread disempowerment. Worse still, it is based on a set of false premises.

The scarcity of goods is a devious and misguided assumption that warrants a competitive plot in which the strong and wise will win out and manage the scarce goods to the benefit of all. For the onetime British prime minister Margaret Thatcher, it's all about letting the market take its course, and with this assertion the dysfunctional economic system becomes a God unto itself.

The highly convoluted system takes quite a degree of unpacking (as indicated by Eisenstein 2011). One significant undercurrent is that humans cannot be trusted with the management of the scarce goods. Why not? Because most humans are fundamentally flawed, which is the reason why the goods are scarce in the first place. So a strategy is needed—not to ensure that the scarce goods are well distributed (that is, dictated by the force of the market) but that the sinful, flawed humans are kept under the control of the wise and mighty.

Keep a close eye on the logic here. Humans, not the goods, are the fundamental problem. And because humans are placed first, the distorted anthropology then ensues in a chain of subsequent distortions, the most outrageous being the claim that the goods are scarce and need to be managed by patriarchal governance. We inhabit a creation with an overflowing *abundance* (more in McFague 2000). Humans knew this for several thousand years before the dark shadow cast by the Agricultural Revolution some ten thousand years ago. *The notion of scarce goods is a corrupt fantasy of the deluded patriarchs.*

Even in the twenty-first century, despite the widespread exploitation of natural resources and the voracious appetite of a population of over 7 billion people, there is still a super-abundance of food and human resources throughout the earth. In parallel with the positive anthropology enunciated by Marianne Williamson in the earlier quote, we can declare that our deepest fear is *not* that our earth is inadequate. *Our deepest fear is that the resources of our earth are powerful beyond measure. It is our light, not our darkness, that most frightens us!* Our inability to make sense of the abundant blessings that surround us has us in the mess we are in.

And of course, our economics and our politics work hand in hand. It is often claimed that politics is all about power, despite the extensive rhetoric of serving the people and seeking to procure the common good. The history of political thought can be traced back to early antiquity, with seminal works such as Plato's *Republic*, Aristotle's *Politics*, and the writings of Confucius. The oldest political institution is that of kingship, itself derived from the roles of clan rulers and chiefs. What made the king distinctly unique was the endowment of divine power. God ruled from above the sky, and ruled down specifically and uniquely through the male king.

Kings, emperors, and other types of monarchs in many countries, including China and Japan, were considered divine. And for the greater part, kingship prevailed until the French Revolution put an end to the divine right of kings. Despite the prevalence of kings and empires, political history as we know it today evolved around the notion of the *polis*, the city-state. Wes Howard-Brook (2016) provides a valuable critique, highlighting that the origin of the state is also closely linked with the art of warfare. Historically speaking, all political communities of the modern type owe their existence to successful warfare.

Ever since the original evolution of kingship, politics involves decision making, governance, and enforcement of law, making laws both civil and criminal in order to preserve law and order. Politics is the pursuit of power, domination, and control. While money has long been associated with the acquisition of power, it was not until the eighteenth century that money was absorbed into the politics of domination. Prior to that time an economic system of exchange of goods—sometimes called a barter economy, at other times, a gift economy—enjoyed extensive popularity.

Adam Smith, whose book *The Wealth of Nations* (1776) became the basis for modern economic theory, proposed that rational self-interest and competition can lead to economic prosperity, above and beyond other models adopting the mutual exchange of goods. Thus was set the basis of the capitalistic value system, the leading paradigm of our time—with several questionable assumptions that go largely uncontested.

Thomas Greco offers the following resume of our current dysfunctional impasse:

> Government and banking have colluded to create a
> political money system that embodies a "debt impera-
> tive" that results in a "growth imperative," which
> forces environmental destruction and rends the social
> fabric while increasing the concentration of power
> and wealth. It creates economic and political insta-
> bilities that manifest in recurrent cycles of depression
> and inflation, domestic and international conflict, and
> social dislocation. (2009, 50)

In this statement we encounter all the wrong moves, which immediately suggests what needs to be altered. Central to any improvement is the notion of a more sustainable econom-ics. This means creating monetary systems and procedures whereby government and banks become more transparent and mutually accountable, and the accountability in question is not merely to human beings. It will also need to involve how natural resources are used, valued, and traded.

Sustainability is quite a complex concept and is often subverted in the functional approaches adopted by financial institutions and governments. As Bernard Lietaer (2001) and Charles Eisenstein (2011) indicate, money is first and foremost a form of energy; how we channel that energy, engage with it, and utilize it cannot be reduced to a set of mechanistic proce-dures in which some control the energy flow on behalf of oth-ers. Most people are not even aware of this basic fact. The big institutions have objectified money into a utilitarian commod-ity, and so have the masses. Both collude in the dysfunctional mess in which we find ourselves.

Sustainability begins with awareness and cannot be advanced without an extensive use of imagination. Every attempt at discerning what an alternative economics might look like emphasizes the need for participation and involvement in financial management. Money should belong first and foremost to people, not to patriarchal financial institutions. Then, as in the barter system of earlier times, people become more aware of the value of money and the value of the goods for which exchanges are being negotiated. People do not think merely in terms of profit and greed; they think in terms of value and mutual enrichment.

The alternative vision goes much deeper and has been lucidly formulated by Charles Eisenstein (2011) in his clarion call to reclaim the significance of money as a medium for gift exchange. Above all else, money denotes *giftedness*, people's desire to gift each other in the service of a deeper and more expansive mutuality. This quality of human regard—with its reconceptualizing of money and its significance—is only possible when humans appreciate the giftedness of the living Earth and all it bestows for our growth and endowment. With this awareness, humans learn to reciprocate for all they have received. Gratitude becomes our default position. Another world can be called into being.

This is not a romantic ideal. For most of human history, humans created and managed their finances in a mutually enriching way. The Bank of England only came into being in 1694, and the first bank in the United States was established in 1781. Banks initially were accountable to the people rather than to governments. The collusive control of the present time between banks and governments is very much an outcome of the twentieth century. Returning financial power to the people is a central responsibility for a more sustainable and effective economics for the future.

The Missing Organicity

Political and economic power today is vested primarily in megacorporations, theoretically accountable to the World Trade Organization (WTO) but effectively a law unto themselves. These transnational corporations operate a globalized trading of goods in a manner that deprives millions of citizens the possibility of empowering and creative engagement. Globalization has evolved through three consecutive phases: cultural, economic, and political. The first and second phases are largely complete, though some protectionism still exists. The final phase has proven to be the most difficult, raising a range of awkward questions about the supremacy of the nation-state.

Globalization has swept across the planet like a tidal wave. Ever since Marshall McLuhan's prediction of the global village, internationality and globalism have come to the fore, and despite the unexpected resistance from nation-states, corporations have proliferated all over planet Earth. Globalization is not just an external socioeconomic phenomenon; it seems to capture an inner human aspiration to become the unified citizens of our one Earth. We can see prototypes in developments such as the unification of China under the Qin Dynasty, the formation of the United States of America, the current experiment known as the European Union, and the likely increase in regional cooperation within the African subcontinent. Taken to its logical conclusion, we may eventually achieve a democratic planetary government.

Such a prospect sounds scary to most people and evokes fear of a new imperial ideology possibly worse than anything we have ever known. Two powerful contemporary forces are at work here—one widely recognized, namely globalization, and the other equally resilient but kept off the ideological radar, namely *localization*. Globalization is an international trade movement mediated through transnational corporations, many of which have their current headquarters in China. By virtue of WTO approval, these corporations are effectively beyond legal sovereignty and control. These corporations exercise no accountability to nation-states, nor are they in any way subject to national laws and controls. In fact they have superseded the nation-state, leaving numerous smaller nations helpless in the face of corporate exploitation and legal exemption.

Corporations have ruthlessly exploited the mineral wealth of several African countries; recklessly altered organic agricultural processes in India, Brazil, and the United States; and commercialized medical resources through pharmaceutical companies that exert extreme pressure on doctors and health-care officials—as evidenced in the massive opposition to the introduction of the US Affordable Care Act of some years ago. The general public, because of slick, manipulative advertising, has become a group of passive and confused consumers in a world of salacious commercialization. It will take substantial adult creativity to reverse this trend.

All is not hopeless, but discerning wisdom is urgently needed, and on a larger scale than thus far available. In a provocatively hope-filled vision, the American social researcher Paul Hawken outlines the hidden but enduring phenomenon of localization. He traces a movement whereby a proliferation of networks arise to serve a vast range of human and cultural needs—on a global scale. Of this movement, Hawken writes,

> The movement can't be divided because it is so atomized—a collection of small pieces, loosely joined. It forms, dissipates, and then re-gathers quickly, without central leadership, command, or control. Rather than seeking dominance, this unnamed movement strives to disperse concentrations of power. It has been capable of bringing down governments, companies, and leaders through witnessing, informing, and massing. The

quickening of the movement in recent years has come
about through information technologies becoming
increasingly accessible and affordable to people every-
where. Its clout resides in its ideas, not in force. . . . The
movement has three basic roots: environmental activ-
ism, social justice initiatives, and indigenous cultures'
resistance to globalization, all of which have become
intertwined. (2007, 12)

Such is the power of networking, a grassroots global
movement that evokes little media attention (because it is not
sensational) and largely suppressed by formal governments
who dread its empowering potential. As major governmental
institutions become more and more ineffective (due to their
usurpation by corporations), and lose the confidence of rank-
and-file citizens (becoming ever more informed and aware),
there is every likelihood that networks will outpace major
institutions. How and when this will happen is difficult to
predict, but it is becoming increasingly clear that the highly
dysfunctional nature of current institutions cannot be sustained in the long term. In time, human creativity will seek
out creative alternatives.

"Your playing small does not serve the world. There is
nothing enlightened about shrinking so that other people will
not feel insecure around you" (Williamson 1992, 190). We
have evolved an economics, politics, and religion based on the
deluded fantasy of playing small. As a species we no longer
know how to honor our adult creativity; we have lost the wisdom of living out of our fuller stature, something we seem to
have integrated more efficiently and creatively in former times.

As indicated several times in this book, our disconnection
from the organic web of life is at the root of most, if not all, the
major problems facing humanity today. The creativity that we
have known for several millennia, and integrated with a large

measure of success, now eludes our grasp. Our objectification of the living Earth itself, especially through our economics, politics, and religion, is the root evil of our age. It was not Satan or some satanic forces on high that plunged us into this mess. We ourselves have created the problem, and it is up to us to redeem ourselves out of it. A failure to do that could well spell the apocalyptic end of *Homo economicus*.

The opening years of the twenty-first century illustrate with a frightening vividness that democracy is on the decline, and a persuasive alternative is nowhere to be seen. The single greatest failure of democracy is the one rarely mentioned and virtually never subjected to critical analysis. I refer to the *erosion of empowering citizenship*. We glamorize the political breakthrough when citizens can openly vote for their governments, whether in South Africa, Burma, or Iraq. No sooner are the elected representatives in office than they begin mitigating or betraying the very promises upon which they were elected. And the voters, in most cases, have no mechanism whatever to call their representatives to accountability. We hail and acclaim the new government, but for the next number of years—four, five, six—we are helpless in the face of betrayal, corruption, and failure to govern in an empowering way. This is what I describe as *immobilized citizenship*.

The middle classes particularly have reacted negatively to populist leaders who appeared to be sliding into authoritarianism, but rather than work to defeat these leaders at the ballot box or strengthen the institutions that could hold them in check, they have ended up supporting military coups or other undemocratic measures. The election of Donald Trump in the United States in 2016 comes to mind. Many Westerners had expected that developing-world democracies like India, Indonesia, South Africa, Brazil, and Turkey would emerge as powerful advocates for democracy and a more empowering brand of politics. But as they've gained power, these emerging democratic giants have acted more like cold-blooded realists. In some cases their own progressive vision brought about their own political regression, Brazil being a glaring example.

Around the globe, democratic meltdowns, not democratic revolutions, now seem to be the norm. From Russia to Venezuela, Thailand, and the Philippines, countries that once appeared to be developing into democracies today seem headed in the other direction. So many countries now remain stuck somewhere between authoritarianism and dysfunctional socialism.

Strategic Alternatives

Two books that can help illuminate our political intransigence are Anne Wilson Schaef's scathing attack in *When Society Becomes an Addict* (1988) and Karen E. Dill's exposition of media propaganda in *How Fantasy Becomes Reality* (2009). Human creativity has been coopted and corrupted, and will only be recovered if and when we choose to name and address the dysfunctionalities that cripple us.

1. Our deluded educational systems are so collusive with the powers that be that most people are no longer capable of critical and creative thinking. We think and behave as the major systems want us to do. In a range of subtle ways we are all falsely imprisoned by media propaganda.

2. Most of the indoctrination today is done in the name of transnational corporations. Most so-called democratic governments are at the mercy of such corporations, who dictate most of our economic, social, medical, and educational values. For instance, in the United States, for every 2.3 doctors there is one pharmaceutical salesperson, which enables us to understand the massive opposition Barack Obama met when he sought to introduce an empowering health bill, and partially explains why his successor, Donald Trump, sought to discard it.

3. To confront the roller-coaster effect of the corporations, humans need new systemic skills largely unknown in our inherited educational systems. Heretofore, the exercise of power has been largely mediated through powerful individuals with rather limited interpersonal structures. We need to shift the focus today to the central role of groups and organizations in our lives and equip ourselves with the collaborative skills that will be needed if we are to transform and redesign the prevailing dysfunctional power structures. Even a spiritual writer like Elizabeth Liebert has identified this crucial resource: "The appearance of structures on a global scale is tantamount to the emergence of a new species on earth. Prior to the last 100 years, there were few examples of global-spanning institutions" (2015, 2).

4. Structures of local government have been weakened significantly and in some cases eradicated entirely around the world. Cutting costs is the usual explanation, but the true cause has much more to do with subtle manipulation of power and domination.

5. The organic relationship with land has been seriously eroded, as more people inhabit urban conglomerates deprived of a convivial relationship with the living earth. This sensuous deprivation weakens our human capacity to create and explore, and to reclaim the more organic relationship with creation that is our natural birthright (more in Abram 2010).

6. Religious idealism has also been undermined, often by the religions themselves, addicted to dualistic splitting (e.g., sacred vs. secular) as they collude extensively with the prevailing powers. The alternative spiritual awakening, sometimes described as a *new mysticism*, has not yet gathered enough momentum to become a transformative influence.

7. Is there a solution to this political cul-de-sac? I believe there is, and in fact it has been evolving organically for some years now. I refer to the power of networking, a social/cultural reframing of social and political engagement, described

in encouraging detail by the American social historian Paul Hawken (2007). It consists of millions of ground-up movements around the world, beavering away at systemic change and empowering the masses, yet not sensational enough to captivate the imagination of our lurid public media (see Hawken 2007, 61–62).

Sociopolitical Empowerment: Gospel Wisdom

The Christian gospel arose from a cultural milieu of oppression and disempowerment. The Roman political colonizers ruled with a firm hand from the top down, often motivated by their own desire for self-aggrandizement. People paid ever increasing taxes first to the Romans, but also for the maintenance of the Jewish temple, itself overseen by imperial force.

While the Christian church has long sought to separate Jesus from political entanglement and maintain a spiritual superiority deemed to be above politics and economics, our contemporary understanding, informed by multidisciplinary research, indicates unambiguously that Jesus engaged directly and subversively with the pressing political and economic challenges of his time. Nowhere is this more clearly illustrated than in his parables.

In the limited space of this book I engage here with just one parable, the exploration of which will alert the reader to a quality of discernment, quite new in our engagement with Scripture. The parable of the Talents as outlined in Matthew 25:14–30 can be remembered even by a little child. As narrated by Matthew, what we actually have is an *allegory*, not a *parable*. And preachers across the centuries have sermonized eloquently on the allegorical message, reminding us to use our talents wisely, indicating the price we will have to pay for failing to do so.

It is unlikely that Jesus told the story in terms of human talents and our responsibility to use them wisely. For a start, the word *talent* had a totally different meaning in the culture of Jesus's time. In its original historical context it denotes a financial measurement, the equivalent of *twenty years' wages for an average worker*. Five talents, therefore, amounts to one hundred years' wages, while two talents equals forty years' wages. And let's not forget that the parable is being told in a social context where the vast majority of people don't have the security of even an annual wage, and the prospect of making a profit as we understand it today was largely unknown.

This discussion brings us to the second cultural feature, largely incomprehensible to our modern capitalistic value system. Many of the early Western philosophers, including Plato, Aristotle, Cato, Cicero, Seneca, and Plutarch, were critics of usury (profit-making). In the legal reforms of the Roman republic (340 BCE), usury and interest were banned. However, in the final period of the republic, the practice was common. Under Julius Caesar (r. 49–44 BCE), a limit of *12 percent* was imposed due to the great number of debtors, and under Justinian law it was set at a mean between 4 percent and 8 percent. Even the Romans denounced excessive profiteering, highlighting the highly subversive nature of the parable of the Talents, unambiguously denouncing the empire, its greed, and its exploitation.

Now imagine yourself among the people hearing this parable. Bring as much as you can of your creative imagination to the narrative context. Situate yourself among a group of people carrying the onus of frequent tax payments to the Roman invaders along with frequent contributions for the priestly maintenance of the temple. These are the same people who, year after year, see more and more of their crops and land produce auctioned off as tax payments. Many are wondering, when and where will it end? Will they be able to hold on to their land, or might a day come when that too will be confiscated? Will they be able to feed themselves and their dependents? Will the male folk be able to find some kind of meaningful work, without which life can become frightening in the extreme?

Many of these people may not be educated in any formal sense, but they are richly endowed with organic agrarian wisdom. They probably know their Hebrew Scriptures better than we often give them credit for. They know what usury means, and they are quick to recognize when it is being flaunted and abused. The very suggestion that somebody makes profit to the tune of 100 percent is utterly obscene; it provokes outrage, anger, and disgust.

We are dealing with a highly subversive narrative evoking shock and dismay in the hearers, encouraging them to become proactive in the pursuit of ecojustice (more in Herzog 1994). The alternative they are offered—the person with the one talent—is indeed ambivalent, but with a prophetic twist that enhances further the subversive intent. He chooses not to collude with the financial exploitation. He opts to become the whistle-blower, calling the brutal landlord to accountability, while exposing the shameful, underhanded tactics: "You reckless bastard: you sow from where you have not reaped and scattered from where you have not scattered"—language that sounds remarkably similar to the prophet Jeremiah.

We then encounter the third guy, maligned and condemned over the centuries as the waster of the talent. Once again let's locate ourselves imaginatively in the cultural context, among listeners to the parable probably hearing it in their native Aramaic. While the Greek translation accuses the talent-owner of burying it in the ground—how does one hide twenty years' wages in the earth?—an alternative translation discerned from the Hebrew is that *he invested his money in the land*. This is exactly what the Torah required and recommended. Now the one commonly portrayed as lazy and fearful emerges as a prophetic liberator with cutting-edge potential. Of course, he will pay the ultimate price, but his story becomes part of the dangerous memory that in time will undermine even the mighty empire itself.

By confusing the parable with the allegory, we end up endorsing the voracious capitalistic system in which God rewards the exploitative hoarders and condemns the one who chose not to collude with the imperial system. On a surface, allegorical interpretation, the person with the one talent is portrayed as ambivalent and cowardly—until we investigate more deeply and see the malicious power games being played out. Now we can see more clearly the subversive irony and sarcasm of the words "Enter into the joy of your master" (Matt. 25:21, 23). The reckless profiteers at the time would have been known as *retainers*—effectively, entrusted slaves. Even though they themselves had been subjected to the humiliation of slavery, in the hope of making it good they often treated their own people as slaves. Yet no matter how much profit they made, or how many of their own folk they cowed into submission, they never rose above the level of being slaves, and as such they were still vulnerable to exploitation and dismissal. *There is no joy for them*—the words are pure sarcasm, in the service of subversive speech.

The evangelists themselves seem to have largely missed the subversive, empowering, liberating message of the parables. Perhaps they knew what the original intention of Jesus was but found it too explosive to retain; instead, they opted for the safer, milder engagement of the allegory. But in doing so, we have betrayed the creative political and economic pedagogy of the oppressed. Amid the complexities of the sociopolitical and economic world of our time, we Christians also fail significantly. We lack that daring, prophetic creativity so foundational to our human destiny and our Christian witness.

Like the person with the one talent, Jesus also paid the ultimate price for his daring and empowering parable-speech. The evangelists began to focus on the price itself—his untimely death—instead of honoring the prophetic witness that led to such a death.

I opened this chapter with an inspiring quote from the social entrepreneur Peter Drucker: "During periods of discontinuous, abrupt change, the essence of adaptation involves a keen sensitivity to what should be abandoned—not what should be changed or introduced. A willingness to depart from the familiar has distinct survival value." Politically and economically we live in times of great dislocation, chaos, and unpredictability about the future. Fear holds many people in its grip, and faced with such uncertain prospects we evidence a strong tendency to regress to a nostalgic past in which we hope all will be safe and well. Such allegiance undermines rather than enhances creative breakthroughs for the future.

In Christian faith we call it the paschal journey, popularly understood as the death and resurrection of Jesus to save humans from their sins; although popular, it is a very poor understanding of a profound theological truth that carries political and economic implications. First, the paschal journey is a declaration that death is an inherent and necessary dimension of all evolutionary growth; without death there cannot be new life.[1] How to recognize the inevitability—even the desirability—of death (in terms of letting go) requires a great deal of discernment. To cling to that which has outlived its usefulness—like the bankrupt economics of our age—merely adds to anomie, disempowerment, and ultimately crippling despair.

---

[1] Accordingly, St. Paul's declaration that death is the consequence of sin (Rom. 6:23), and therefore an evil to be got rid of, is an understanding devoid of evolutionary context. It is a dangerously misleading claim.

Our world today is inundated in layers of meaningless death, often arising from sheer ignorance about the meaning and necessity of death. For instance, Charles Eisenstein (2011) points out that we have assigned to money an immortal value. Contrary to all the organic processes of the natural world, we don't allow money to die out—in other words, to lose its economic value after a certain period of time. Consequently, we have deified money above and beyond all natural processes in creation, assigning to money a God-like status that translates into another form of divine imperialism, instead of being a resource to be deployed in accordance with human creativity.

Without diminution, decline, and death, new life becomes impossible. It is a universal law of all creation and a linchpin around which evolution revolves. The misunderstanding of death's role has largely arisen from the patriarchal religions, and from Christianity in particular. Its integral significance continues to be poorly understood, even among theologians. The true creativity of Jesus is not in his redemptive death but in his subversive, prophetic life. We need to rethink anew the death of the historical Jesus and re-vision its role to empower new life and possibility. We take up this challenge in the next chapter.

8

Beyond the Violent Redemption

Since the moment Constantine made the cross his personal talisman, the sign under which his troops would always win, the cross has been the symbol of both martyrdom and murder. Soldiers' declaration that they are willing to die for the cause also always buys them a license to kill for it.

—Stephen J. Patterson

For popular Christianity, creativity is a distraction from the real issues that should engage us as people of faith, specifically the fact that humans are fundamentally flawed, and from a Christian point of view nothing short of the cross of Jesus can guarantee a creative—that is, a salvific—outcome. Moreover, the happiness that comes from the exercise of creativity can never be obtained in this perverted vale of tears. It can only be achieved through the salvation of the promised life hereafter, and that becomes available primarily through the power of the death and resurrection of Jesus. Whatever creativity means, it certainly is not available on this side of eternity; perhaps it can be obtained in the life hereafter.

Exaggerated? It depends who you converse with. For an evangelical Christian, the type that tends to take the Bible literally—and there are millions of them around the world—this is what they believe. So do millions of others, whom we might describe as rank-and-file Christians (especially in the southern hemisphere). And there is no shortage of ardent preachers eager to deliver this fear-filled message. Progressive Christians, who comprise millions rather than thousands strongly reject such a pessimistic view. These are the ones who have moved from the old understanding and now embrace a different quality of hope. Many others—again in the millions rather than thousands, have walked away. What's the point in trying if one is doomed from the start?

I describe the landscape with these rather graphic images because it depicts the baggage that has done irreparable damage to millions of people and, more seriously, has severely undermined the God-given creativity I highlight in the present work. So, where did it all go so wrong for human creativity?

The Foundational Perversion

According to the book of Genesis, it all began well. God saw everything as good—and creative—and in God's eyes it was all meant to flourish, with humans almost at the pinnacle of the creative prerogative. That is Genesis 1, with the Spirit breathing over the chaotic, creative emptiness, followed by the Creator, sounding the repeating, empowering mantra: "Let it Be!"

The God of Genesis 1 seems like a gentle, facilitating, and animating Deity, quite at home with everything in creation, including humans. The whole tenor of the creative imperative changes when we move to Genesis 2. Here we are dealing with the LORD God, an imperial kyriarchal figure who seems to like ordering everything as he dictates. We detect echoes of the patriarchal urge to control. Very quickly the dysfunctional human (and the violent God) comes to the surface.

The tree in the center of the garden (Genesis 2–3) is replete with ancient echoes of creative abundance. In all probability it represents the Great Earth Mother Goddess for whom the tree was a primary symbol in ancient times. The woman takes the fruit from the tree. She has been doing it for millennia, women being the traditional pioneers of agricultural development, a fact widely recognized today. She knows exactly what she is doing, honoring her fertile womb, her nourishing heart, and her vast reservoirs for creative abundance.

Had we stayed with the female prerogative, there would have been no problem—at least not the moralistic and theological quagmires we now encounter. We would have a very different economics, politics, and religion. The divine creative imperative would be at the fore, as it had been for many previous millennia.

As we now know, the Agricultural Revolution was largely triggered by climate change, with dehydration ravaging the fertile plains of North Africa and Saudi Arabia, changing them into the vast deserts we see today (Taylor 2005). The cultural panic-reaction gave birth to our patriarchal system, which is primarily at play in Genesis 2–3. The petrified, reactionary male has lost all trust in the fertility of the Great Mother. He now lives in a state of deep alienation, to a point that he cannot even recognize the fruitfulness of the earth, never mind be able to receive it from the tree of life. And in the cruelest twist of all, he subverts and undermines the woman's fertile potential (read: creativity).

Salvation from Alienation

About two hundred thousand years ago our ancestors migrated from Northeast Africa, up through the Middle East, and into

various parts of Europe. They came to be known as the Neanderthals, who often lived in cold, arid conditions with much of
Europe covered with ice at that time. Long regarded as brutish
and somewhat primitive, more recent research indicates that
the Neanderthals were highly adaptable and innovative, with
some sophisticated communication skills, a sense of social solidarity, and an intriguing capacity for ritual-making (especially
regarding the burial of the dead). Their rather sudden disap-
pearance still remains a great mystery.

The icy conditions of Europe then progressively moved
south and eventually affected North Africa, where, according
to Steve Taylor (2005), modern aggressive agriculture radically
changed the course of human evolution. The weather patterns
in North Africa seem to have unfolded as follows:

- 22,000–10,500 years ago: The Sahara was devoid of
  any human occupation outside the Nile Valley and
  extended 250 miles farther south than it does today.
- 10,500–9,000 years ago: Monsoon rains begin
  sweeping into the Sahara, transforming the region
  into a habitable area swiftly settled by Nile Valley
  dwellers.
- 9,000–7,300 years ago: Continued rains, vegetation
  growth, and animal migrations lead to well-established human settlements, including the introduction
  of domesticated livestock such as sheep and goats.
- 7,300–5,500 years ago: Retreating monsoon rains ini-
  tiate progressive dehydration (known as *desiccation*),
  creating severe drought in what is currently known as
  the Sahara Desert along with the desert region of Saudi
  Arabia (hence, Taylor's [2005] naming of *Saharasia*).
  Extensive human dislocation ensues, leading to the
  streamlining and restructuring of land, to the benefit of
  dominant males.

The objectification and commodification of land had already come to the fore along the northern and eastern Mediterranean coastlines. It now became a dominant cultural pattern, creating a psychic breach between humans and the organic web of life. For several previous millennia, it seems that humans saw themselves as integral to the natural world. Human self-understanding was defined in terms of what humans belonged to. With the establishment of the Agricultural Revolution, all that changed. The earth and the land now became material objects for humans to conquer and control. Alienation became a cultural norm, endorsed by all the formal religions, and unambiguously reinforced by the monotheistic religions.

While the politics and economics of the day sought to commodify and objectify the land, and the patriarchal rulers made it an object for conflict and later for warfare, the dominant patriarchal religions problematized the land as embodying the countervalues of all that was holy, sacred, and of the Spirit of God. Close attention to the land and love for it were declared to be distractions from the things of God, a source of temptation that would undermine humanity's true destiny for spiritual maturity. For the monotheistic religions in particular, escape from our entrapment in the land was the surest route to salvation with God in a world hereafter.

Classical Greek philosophy reinforced this foundational alienation by setting up a whole range of dualistic splits, the better known being earth vs. heaven, matter vs. spirit, body vs. soul. Human beings were declared to be ensouled (by Aristotle), and while animals were also ensouled the human endowment was undoubtedly superior to any other creature. (In fact, for Aristotle it is the capacity for rationality that makes us superior.) By thus elevating humans, our worth and dignity were undermined rather than advanced. Our exalted separation from the web of life alienated us in every sphere of our existence.

For the great Eastern religions, the resolution to human alienation is the achievement of nirvana, the escape from the karmic cycle of birth and death. For both Hinduism and Buddhism, nirvana doesn't just happen when you die, and when you die you don't necessarily reach nirvana. Nirvana is a state of mind, the ultimate enlightenment, the great awakening from the deceit of this existence. The ultimate release is known as *parinirvana*, a state of final fulfillment, the precise nature of which is described neither by Hinduism nor Buddhism.

The notion of an afterlife, and redemption therein, came into Judaism at a rather late stage. The Torah and Talmud alike focus on the purpose of earthly life, which is to fulfill one's duties to God and one's fellow man. Succeeding at this brings reward; failure brings punishment. Whether rewards and punishments continue after death, or whether anything at all happens after death, is not as important. Despite the subject's general exclusion from the Jewish sacred texts, however, Judaism does incorporate views on the afterlife. Yet unlike the other monotheistic religions, no one view has ever been officially agreed upon, leaving much room for speculation.

Christianity and Islam place much emphasis on reward in the hereafter for the good life and damnation for sinners. For Christianity the real grip of sin and its alienation is an inherited condition from the original sin of Adam and Eve. For Christians the death of Jesus disrupts or breaks that vicious cycle, providing a special divine "resource" called *grace* through which humans stand a better chance of obtaining salvation in a world hereafter. It is the death of Jesus more than anything else that resolves the alienation.[1]

---

[1] Strictly speaking, the alienation is never resolved; it continues to haunt people until the end of their lives.

Christianity's Violent Cross

Christianity borrowed from Judaism the notion of a sacrificial lamb through which the inherited alienation could be resolved. The Jewish Day of Atonement—the celebration of Yom Kippur (Lev. 16:1–34; 23:26–32; Num. 29:7–11)—marked the breakthrough into new freedom and hope. John Shelby Spong (2007; 2016) persuasively argues that it is our Gentile-inherited tendency to literalize events like Yom Kippur—frequently distorting the original Jewish context—that leaves us with a grossly convoluted understanding of atonement, in both the Old Testament setting and in its application to the death of Jesus.

There is the additional factor complicating our allurement to the notion of atonement, namely the phenomenon of *scapegoating* (see the valuable elaboration in Girard 1986 and Campbell 2013). It describes how a person or group is forced to carry blame for others or to suffer in their place. Derived from the Old Testament (Lev. 16:8ff.), a goat is let loose in the wilderness during Yom Kippur after the high priest symbolically laid the sins of the people on its head. Jesus is clearly projected onto this role, even to the perverse level that the phenomenon of scapegoating becomes synonymous with sacralized violence. We too easily forget that Jesus was killed because he posed a threat to Roman and Jewish imperialism, not as a divine scapegoat sent to rescue sinful humanity.

St. Paul is the primary architect of salvation through the power of the cross. Pauline scholars tend to argue that it is the resurrection of Jesus rather than his death on the cross that guarantees breakthrough and salvation. Nonetheless, for Paul the cross and resurrection are inseparably entwined, and whatever Paul's original intention might have been, historically the cross dominates the Christian landscape. The death of Jesus becomes almost an end in itself, seriously subverting the life of

Jesus and the breakthrough of the God's new reign (the new Companionship of Empowerment) inviting all Christians and others into an empowering creative endeavor that radically transforms our inherited notions of salvation and redemption.

We need to engage in a more direct and discerning manner on what exactly the death of Jesus means within the context of his empowering mission, one that posed a huge threat to the Roman imperial forces of the day. As his popularity grew and crowds began to follow, it appears that substantial numbers of people felt a sense of communal empowerment.[2] This may have turned some into potential violent revolutionaries who might have joined the Zealots, but the evidence points more toward

---

[2] The crowd following Jesus at the end seems to consist of the same people who followed him for much of his public ministry, and probably included many who were healed, welcomed to the open table, and empowered through his subversive words and deeds. It is widely assumed that they betrayed him in the end, and worse still called for his crucifixion (Mark 15:11–13). While Mark highlights their role with five distinct references, both Matthew and Luke reduce the allusions to three; John only retains a single reference (12:12–18). Borg and Crossan (2006) pretty much single-handedly challenged this popular view, suggesting that the negative portrayal of the crowd is a politically motivated distortion of the facts in order, first, to deflect attention from the Romans (and their collusion with Jewish authorities), and second, to validate the punitive actions of the authorities, insinuating that even the people themselves wanted to get rid of this dangerous rebel. Borg and Crossan (2006, 88–90, 144) highlight the fact that throughout the Holy Week narrative of Mark's Gospel the crowd consistently adopts a protective role: on Sunday (Mark 11:8), Monday (Mark 11:18), Tuesday (Mark 11:32; 12:12, 37). They distinguish between the faithful crowd and a much smaller group (located in Herod's palace) stirred up by the authorities to seek Jesus's execution. Jesus was arrested in the darkness apart from his large protective crowd and was crucified as swiftly as possible. Historians generally agree that the story of Pilate offering the crowd a choice of releasing Barabbas or Jesus (see Mark 15:6–15), with the crowd seeking the freedom of Barabbas, is considered to be fictitious. There is no non-Christian reference to the strange practice of giving complete amnesty to a prisoner—*any* prisoner chosen by a crowd—on festival days.

a growing sense of self-confidence in the face of the excessive taxation that had to be paid both to the Romans and for the upkeep of the Jerusalem temple. People probably continued to pay taxes as best they could, but increasingly began to reimagine what an alternative society might begin to look like, as Jesus vividly illustrated in the parables, the healing events, and sharing at the common table. Not merely were people better able to endure their plight of hardship and struggle, they began to grow into the nonviolent wisdom of how to change life for the better. In a word, the people were being *empowered* to overcome and transform their internalized oppression.

This transformative change—at once psychological, spiritual, social, and political—began to scare the authorities. They quickly realized that they were dealing with a subversive revolutionary who in time could pose a serious threat to Roman hegemony. They set out to capture him, and if possible eliminate him. And they succeeded, condemning him to crucifixion, a form of death specifically for subversives who posed a threat to Roman imperialism.

The Gospel writers pick up the story that began to emerge among the early Christians as they struggled to make sense of the sudden violent end to which Jesus was subjected. They began to draw inspiration from their inherited Jewish faith, and quite quickly Jesus came to be identified with the sacrificial lamb of former times. Paul championed the death (and resurrection) of Jesus as the only gospel that mattered (1 Cor. 15:1–4); he had no interest in the life of Jesus with its empowering strategies of parabolic story, healing, and commensality (the common table). Building on the popular folklore of the fallen but exalted hero, the Gospel writers created a highly dramatic glamorization of pain, suffering, and death on the cross, contextualized within the imperial court and the tense atmosphere of frenetic political figureheads, all culminating in a grand finale for the imperial Christ. And amid such glamorized violence and imperial propaganda, the harsh subversive truth—along with its unconquerable creativity—was almost totally lost.

In all probability, there were no trials (despite the elaborate Gospel accounts), nor little involvement of high imperial figureheads (Herod, Pilate, etc.). Having been seized by the military, with or without a Judas-betrayal, Jesus was given a quick, brutal death on a cross. It was probably all over before either his family or disciples knew about it. Horrified and shocked by what had happened, the disciples (particularly the Twelve) ran for their lives, and in all probability they did not come back, as Luke in the opening chapters of Acts leads us to believe.

The meager traces of enduring fidelity belong to a small group led by a brave and creative woman known as Mary Magdalene, the one acclaimed by St. Augustine as the Apostle to the Apostles. It seems that this was predominantly a female group, although likely consisting of males as well. This group became the foundation stone of the early church, a community of faith formed around several creative women (and some men), which, after almost two thousand years, Christianity is beginning to acknowledge and reclaim (see Schüssler Fiorenza 1983; Osiek & MacDonald 2006; Malone 2014). Only when the truth of this original bedrock group comes to full light will Christianity know its resurrection breakthrough. Only then will justice be done and will Christian creativity stand a better chance of coming into its own.

The exaltation of the fallen hero translates into the resurrection narratives of the Gospels. In a culture where creative imagination frequently morphed into visions and ecstatic states, it is both possible and likely that the disillusioned, heartbroken followers (particularly the women) did experience a nearness and intimacy of Jesus in their lives. Such "encounters" were not merely hallucinations, but neither were they physical-type appearances. What ensued was an experiential conviction that Jesus was more alive after his death than even during his earthly life. What happened to Jesus we don't know, and probably never will; nor does it really matter. What does matter is the empowering transformation of the first followers (especially the women), those in whom Jesus was truly risen and through whom the empowering message of the gospel would spread throughout the whole creation.

The Nonviolent Revolution

Christianity is a highly creative religion. It centers on an empowering companionship, described in the Gospels as the kingdom of God. In a world so inundated in violence and imperial contagion, Christianity stands out with a bold, alternative vision. Central to that vision is the subtle, enduring force of *nonviolence*, precisely the dimension that has been so tragically neglected, disowned, and subverted.

Several important studies highlight this neglected dimension of Jesus's life and ministry (see works by Lisa Sowle Cahill, André Trocmé, Walter Wink, John Dear, and Terrence J. Rynne). The perennial text supporting the notion of a nonviolent Jesus is that of "Love your enemies and pray for those who persecute you" (Matt. 5:43). The Catholic scholar John P. Meier (2009, 531, 550, 573) claims that neither in the Old Testament, Qumran literature, or in the intertestamental writings is there any equivalent to this unambiguous, forthright love of one's adversary. In other words, it seems unique to Christianity.

In fact, the entire Sermon on the Mount can be viewed as a Magna Carta for gospel nonviolence, and the unique insights of the late Walter Wink are frequently cited as a foundational biblical basis for the nonviolence of Jesus and the Christian faith:

> The God whom Jesus reveals refrains from all forms
> of reprisal and demands no victims. God does not

endorse holy wars or just wars or religions of violence. The reign of God means the complete and definitive elimination of every form of violence between
individuals and nations. Yet, Jesus was not passive in
the face of injustice and evil. To the contrary Jesus
reveals a way to fight evil with all our power without becoming violent ourselves. *It is a way—the only
way possible—of not becoming what we hate.* Jesus
abhors both passivity and violence. He articulates, out
of the history of his own people's struggles, a way by
which evil can be opposed without being mirrored,
the oppressor resisted without being emulated, and
the enemy neutralized without being destroyed. (Wink
1992, 149, 189)

Three memorable injunctions occur in Matthew's Sermon
on the Mount that for Walter Wink capture the nonviolent
vision of Jesus: "Do not resist one who is evil. But if anyone
strikes you on the right cheek, turn to him the other also; and
if anyone would sue you and take your coat, let him have your
cloak as well; and if anyone forces you to go one mile, go with
him two miles" (Matt. 5:39–41). The statements are loaded
with irony and parody, and the richly nuanced meaning can
easily escape the average hearer.

Wink illustrates lucidly and vividly the countercultural
nonviolent dynamic:

1. *"If anyone strikes you on the right cheek ..."*

Why the *right* cheek? A blow by the right fist in that right-
handed world would land on the *left* cheek of the opponent.
An open-handed slap would also strike the left cheek. To hit
the right cheek with a fist would require using the left hand.
The only way one could naturally strike the right cheek with
the right hand would be with the back of the hand. We are
dealing here with insult, not a fistfight. The intention is clearly

not to injure but to humiliate, to put someone in his or her place. A backhand slap was the usual way of admonishing inferiors. Masters backhanded slaves; husbands, wives; parents, children; men, women; Romans, Jews. We have here a set of unequal relations, in each of which retaliation would invite retribution. The only normal response would be cowering submission. Why then does he counsel those already humiliated people to turn the other cheek? *Because this action robs the oppressor of the power to humiliate.* The person who turns the other cheek is saying, in effect, "Try again. Your first blow failed to achieve its intended effect. I deny you the power to humiliate me. I am a human being just like you. Your status does not alter that fact. You cannot demean me." (Wink 1992, 175–76)

Such a response would create enormous difficulties for the striker. Logistically, how would he hit the other cheek now turned to him? He cannot backhand it with his right hand (one only need try this to see the problem). If he hits with a fist, he makes the other his equal, acknowledging him as a peer. But the point of the back of the hand is to reinforce institutionalized inequality. Even if the dominant one orders that the other person should be flogged for such cheeky behavior, the point has been irrevocably made. Notice has been given that this subordinate is in fact a human being. In that world of honor and shaming, the dominator has been rendered impotent to instill shame on a subordinate. He has been stripped of his power to dehumanize the other. As Gandhi taught, "The first principle of nonviolent action is that of noncooperation with everything humiliating."

2. *"If anyone would sue you for your outer garment . . ."* Matthew and Luke disagree whether it is the outer garment (Luke) or the undergarment (Matthew) that is being seized. But the Jewish practice of giving the outer garment as a pledge (it alone would be useful as a blanket for sleeping) makes it clear

that Luke's order is correct, even though he does not preserve the legal setting.

Indebtedness was endemic in first-century Palestine (more in Fiensy 2014). Jesus's parables are full of debtors struggling to salvage their lives. Heavy debt was not, however, a natural calamity that had overtaken the incompetent. It was the direct consequence of Roman imperial policy. It is to this situation that Jesus speaks. His hearers are the poor and disenfranchised. They share a rankling hatred for a system that subjects them to humiliation by stripping them of their lands, their goods, finally even their outer garments.

Why then does Jesus counsel them to give over their undergarments as well? This would mean stripping off all their clothing and marching out of court stark naked. Nakedness was taboo in Judaism, and shame fell less on the naked party than on the person viewing or causing the nakedness (Gen. 9:20–27). In his now naked state, the debtor has brought the creditor under the same prohibition that led to the curse of Canaan. Imagine him leaving the court, naked, his friends and neighbors, disgusted and angry, join his growing procession, which now resembles a victory parade. Imagine the guffaws that would ensue. There stands the creditor, covered with shame, the poor debtor's outer garment in the one hand, his undergarment in the other. The tables have suddenly been turned on the creditor. The debtor had no hope of winning the case; the law was entirely in the creditor's favor. But the poor man has transcended the plight of humiliation. He has risen above shame. At the same time he has registered a stunning protest against the system that created his debt in the first place.

Jesus provides here a hint of how to take on the entire system by unmasking its essential cruelty and burlesquing its pretensions to justice. Here is a poor man who will no longer be treated as a sponge to be squeezed dry by the rich. He accepts the laws as they stand, pushes them to absurdity, and reveals them for what they have become. He strips naked, walks out before his fellows, and leaves this creditor, and the whole economic edifice he represents, stark naked.

3. *"Go the second mile."* Jesus's third example is drawn from the relatively enlightened practice of limiting the amount of forced or impressed labor that Roman soldiers could levy on subject peoples to a single mile. Such forced service was a constant feature in Palestine from Persian to late Roman times. This forced labor was a source of bitter resentment by all Roman subjects. It is in this context of Roman military occupation that Jesus speaks. He does not counsel revolt. One does not "befriend" the soldier, draw him aside, and drive a knife into his back. Jesus was surely aware of the futility of armed insurrection against Roman imperial might; he certainly did nothing to encourage those whose hatred of Rome was near to flaming into violence.

But why carry his pack a second mile? Is this not to rebound to the opposite extreme of aiding and abetting the enemy? Not at all. The question here, as in the two previous instances, is how the oppressed can recover the initiative and assert human dignity in a situation that cannot for the time being be changed. The rules are Caesar's, but how one responds to the rules is God's, and Caesar has no power over that.

Imagine then the soldier's surprise when, at the next mile marker, he reluctantly reaches to assume his pack, and the civilian says, "Oh no, let me carry it another mile." Why would he want to do that? What is he up to? Normally, soldiers have to coerce people to carry their packs, but this Jew does so cheerfully, and will not stop! From a situation of servile docility, the oppressed have once more seized the initiative. They have taken back the power of choice. The soldier is thrown off balance by being deprived of the predictability of his victim's response. He has never dealt with such a problem before. Now he has been forced into making a decision for which nothing in his previous experience has prepared him. If he has enjoyed feeling superior to the vanquished, he will not enjoy it today. Imagine the situation of a Roman infantryman pleading with a Jew to give back his pack!

The humor of this scene may have escaped us, but it could scarcely have been lost on Jesus's hearers, who must have been regaled at the prospect of thus disempowering their oppressors. Jesus does not encourage Jews to walk a second mile in order to build up merit in heaven, exercise a supererogatory piety, or kill the soldier with kindness. He is helping an oppressed people find a way to protest and neutralize an onerous practice despised throughout the empire. He is not giving a nonpolitical message of spiritual world-transcendence. He is formulating a worldly spirituality in which the people at the bottom of society or under the thumb of imperial power learn to recover their humanity.

To those whose lifelong pattern has been to cringe before their masters, Jesus offers a way to liberate themselves from servile actions and a servile mentality. And he asserts that they can do this before there is a revolution. There is no need to wait until Rome has been defeated, or peasants are landed and slaves freed. They can begin to behave with dignity and a recovered sense of humanity now, even under the unchanged conditions of the old order. Jesus's sense of divine immediacy has social implications. The reign of God—the new Companionship of Empowerment—is already breaking into the world, and it comes not as an imposition from on high but as the leaven slowly causing the dough to rise (Matt. 13:33; Luke 13:20–21). Jesus's teaching on nonviolence is thus of a piece with his proclamation of the dawning new reign of God.

Parabolic Creativity

Jesus worked to relieve the underlying causes of the Jews' suffering, particularly the structural and cultural violence built into their political system. He did so with remarkable ingenuity, creativity, and originality. Nowhere is this more visible than in the parables, with the provocative opening invitation: Imagine . . .

In the parable stories, Jesus parodies and seeks to undermine many prevailing structural assumptions. In all cases he invites the hearers to reimagine an alternative liberating praxis centered on structural reform, alternative use of resources (especially land), and the pursuit of justice. The evangelists themselves handle the parables quite poorly, interpreting the highly subversive stories as allegories rather than parables.[3] I am much more persuaded by the Scripture scholar William Herzog, who wrote that the foundational stories told by Jesus were actually narratives of subversive speech, effectively creating a pedagogy of the oppressed as expounded in the mid-twentieth century by the Brazilian social activist, Paulo Freire.

"The parable, then," writes William Herzog, "was not primarily a vehicle to communicate theology or ethics, but a codification designed to stimulate social analysis and to expose the contradictions between the actual situation of its hearers and the Torah of God's justice" (1994, 28). This is gospel creativity at its finest, most original, subtle, subversive, liberating, and

---

[3] The word *allegory* derives from the Greek *allegoria* (speaking otherwise). It uses a given story to convey or teach religious or moral lessons, or it interprets elements of the given story to illuminate religious meaning. For instance, Matt. 22:1–14 (Luke 14:15–24) describes a king giving a feast for his son, often interpreted allegorically with the king representing God and the son being Jesus. Royal appellations are being employed that are difficult to reconcile with the nonimperial Jesus.

empowering—and posing an unmistakable threat to Roman and Jewish imperialism alike.

Furthermore, by viewing the miracle stories not as some supernatural signs of Jesus's divinity but as parables in action, we detect the same creative empowerment at work. In Mark 3:1–5 Jesus has healed a man with a withered hand on the Sabbath. It is stunning to read what happens next: "The Pharisees went out and immediately conspired with the Herodians against [Jesus], how to destroy him." (Mark 3:6). Already in the third chapter of Mark's Gospel, Jesus is marked for the gibbet. Why? What had he done? He had taken action to challenge structures that dehumanized, diminished, and destroyed, including a system where the disabled were regarded as unholy. For Jesus, the rules and regulations didn't matter: the healing and transformative wholeness must not be delayed. Jesus could not abide exclusion, separation, and hatred of the enemy. Parables of word and parables of action (miracles) both catalyze a new and daring resolution.

In the conditions of first-century Palestine, a political revolution against the Romans could only be catastrophic, as the events of 66–73 CE would prove. Jesus does not propose armed revolution. But he does lay the foundations for a revolution that had transformative social, political, and economic power. In speaking truth to power, Jesus was awakening depths of human creativity that could shake and destabilize any empire. The subversive creativity encountered several obstacles, the untimely death of Jesus himself being the first, and recurring religious persecution. In time the empire faded, and subversive Christianity survived despite several ecclesiastical attempts to tame its insatiable creativity.

What the present chapter has sought to highlight, more than anything else, is the creative liberation of the entire life of Jesus, often overshadowed by the exaggerated importance of his death. Such a death was the consequence of a life radically and richly lived, unique for its subversive, empowering intent. Salvific breakthrough belongs primarily to the life of Jesus and not to his death. Suffering for the sake of suffering, martyrlike self-immolation, has no place in this dispensation.

Creative commitment to breaking the chains of oppression and injustice will involve many types of suffering, as happened for Jesus and for every prophetic visionary. These belong to the daily challenges and undertakings involved in the liberation and empowerment of the new Companionship of Empowerment, and not merely to the heroic death that may eventually ensue. It is the unheroic but persistent loyalty to a world made new that characterizes every authentic spirituality. Enduring breakthrough and the empowering hope that ensues are built on the foundations of an entire life, not merely on the witness of a remarkable death.

9

Toward a Spiritual Revolution

*The mystic is a religious anarchist and utopian, who
speaks for an ancient tradition of protest against religious alienation. The mystic tries to undermine the law,
and to create religious happiness by melting God down.*

—Don Cupitt

Religious practice is an extremely complex field, subject to a
quality of analysis that illuminates the landscape in a very limited way. Western media tend to portray religion as archaic,
outdated, and irrelevant. Several academics, particularly those
committed to rational science, tend to support this view,
although many of them claim to have totally abandoned religion. The abandonment of religion (or church) is itself a complex issue, since millions who have left religion behind have
adopted, to one degree or another, various spiritual or esoteric
practices. Arguably religion is in decline, while the search for
spiritual meaning continues unabated.

What deserves a more discerning analysis is the amorphous
nature of the religious landscape on a universal scale, above
and beyond the monopoly on rationality claimed by the West.

Much of the African subcontinent exhibits a sense of religious celebration with huge empowering potential, particularly for the poor and marginalized; more extensive and thorough research would confirm the same for many parts of Asia, and for the Latinos in both South and North America. And let's not jump too quickly to the Marxist conclusion that in many of these situations religion is an opium of the people, keeping them sane and marginally fulfilled in debilitating conditions.

So, we have a great deal of religiosity, some popularized and esoteric, more formally organized in a structured and ritualized way, and a minority who have abandoned religion completely (according to themselves). As with most features of our postmodern world, the picture is fluid, flexible, and open to several articulations. My interest is in the subgroup who embrace religion in a creative way, characterized by great freedom, a desire for exploration, a movement beyond dogmatism, and eagerness for something akin to mystical experience. My conviction is that this is the niche where creativity is likely to flourish best.

Mysticism has had a checkered history. Probably the oldest religion known to humans, mysticism has morphed over several evolutionary breakthroughs. Currently, it characterizes much of the environmental movement and the emerging ecological consciousness (see Abram 2010; Christie 2013); it attracts millions of people to solitude, stillness, and contemplative prayer, usually described as meditation. At more subtle levels it manifests in a range of alternative networks, whether dealing with the fertility of the land, the health of the human body, or the well-being of the human spirit. The opening quote from Don Cupitt alerts us to one countercultural dimension of contemporary mysticism: humans tend not to entertain alienation for long.

In a previous work (O'Murchu 2012), I outlined the largely unexplored realm of the Great Spirit as articulated universally in the spirituality of indigenous, tribal peoples. In this long ignored and often demonized faith system, we detect a fresh appreciation of spirituality that can aptly be described as Spirit-encountering-spirit. Because dualistic splitting is so endemic to monotheistic religion, not only is there little possibility of acknowledging a Spirit-spirit connection, but the very notion is deemed to be heretical and a threat to religious orthodoxy.

For formal religion generally, and especially for the monotheistic faiths, *spirit* denotes a quality of divine preexistence, totally at variance with our human, earthly condition. Spirit belongs to God and can only be experienced by the human in a very limited way, which itself is only possible through a special grace of God. For formal religion these distinctions must be kept crystal clear.

Creativity "ex Profundis"

While Christianity acknowledges a creative role of the Spirit in the initial stages of creation (Gen. 1:1), the fullness of the Spirit is not conferred on humans until after Pentecost as described in Acts 2:1–11, and each Christian receives the Spirit through the sacrament of Baptism. For indigenous belief systems, on the other hand, Spirit denotes the primordial creative energy that births everything into existence, humans included. This foundational life force is transpersonal, not merely personal. According to Genesis 1:1–2, it is the foundational, original life force, arising *ex profundis* (rather than *ex nihilo*), without beginning or end. It is the divine wellspring of all creativity, in whose name everything is declared to be good. And the goodness complexifies according to a creative imperative (a divine eroticism), forever impregnating and sustaining universal life in its multiple diverse expressions.

Consequently, humans, despite their sinfulness, are fundamentally grounded in the creative energy of that same creative

Spirit. And not merely are we grounded in the Spirit, we are forever yearning to connect more meaningfully. Spirit forever seeks out spirit, and it is in that creative synthesis that evolution thrives and flourishes.

Within that creative process, however, there also exists the great universal paradox of creation-cum-destruction, otherwise known as the cycle of birth-death-rebirth. Without that contradictory paradox, life as we know it would cease completely. I elaborate on this foundational paradox throughout the present work. Suffice it to note here that we are dealing with a *paradox* that should not be dismissed or denounced as evil, or as a fundamental flaw. It is an integral dimension of all creation, human life included.

The core argument of this chapter unfolds as follows:

- Spirituality understood as Spirit-encountering-spirit predates formal religions by several thousand years.
- Spirituality, more than religion, is capable of honoring the ancient incarnational creativity being explored in the present work.
- The spirituality of indigenous tribal peoples, specifically their faith in the Great Spirit, provides an important contemporary aperture into our ancient spirit-inspired creativity.
- In light of all the above, the creativity embedded in the opening chapters of the book of Genesis needs to be reclaimed, rehabilitated, and articulated afresh.

Creative Spirit at Work in Creation

I begin with the last point, a fresh reading of Genesis (chapters 1 and 2 specifically), highlighting the foundational role of the Spirit as the primary agent infusing and sustaining every creative dimension of creation, human and nonhuman alike. Let's begin with the strangely suggestive text from Proverbs:

> The LORD possessed me in the beginning of his way, before his works of old. I was set up from everlasting, from the beginning, before ever the earth was. When there were no depths, I was brought forth; when there were no fountains abounding with water. While as yet he had not made the earth, nor the fields, nor the highest part of the dust of the world. When he prepared the heavens, I was there: when he set a compass upon the face of the deep, when he established the clouds above, when he gave to the sea his decree, that the waters should not pass his commandment, when he appointed the foundations of the earth, I was there beside him, as one brought up with him. And I was daily his delight, rejoicing always before him. (Prov. 8:22–30)[1]

The passage requires the spiritual seeker to ask a number of basic questions, ones that are nonetheless foundational to the deeper discernment I am seeking to honor throughout this book:

- Who is this One watching all that happens?
- Who was this One who seems to have been there *before* the Creator?
- Why do we Christians put the Creator first?

---

[1] This is a complex and controversial passage, with Lady Wisdom declaring herself to be a life force of unique originality, possibly predating the one we call the Creator. Possible parallels with ancient Goddess notions are reviewed by Kloppenborg (1982), while Scripture scholar Alan Lenzi (2006) provides a comprehensive overview of how the passage has been interpreted in the scholarly world.

- Can we discern in a deeper way who is this someone
  (some force?) who empowers the Creator to do the work
  of creating?

In responding to these questions, we can begin by noting
the underlying Hebrew/Aramaic meaning of some key words
and phrases being employed. The Hebrew word for beginning
is *b'reshit*, rendering Genesis 1:1 as follows: "In the beginning of God's preparing the heavens and the earth . . ." Other
translations are possible and today may be considered more
appropriate:

- "In the beginning when God created the heavens and
  the earth . . ."
- "When God began creating the heavens and the
  earth . . ."
- "In the beginning of God's creating . . ."

And consider this translation from the original Hebrew:
"At the beginning of God's creating of the heavens and the
earth, when the earth was wild and waste (*tohu va-vohu*),
darkness over the face of the ocean, breath of God hovering
over the face of the waters, God said: Let there be light" (Fox
1983, 11).

Beginnings are always taking place, without necessarily marking a definitive newness. Infinite creative possibilities open out from the formlessness, the undifferentiated and
bottomless abyss of primordial chaos (similar to the modern
scientific notion of the multiverse). There is great depth and
darkness to life, and it is a fertile darkness, or what quantum
physics names as the *creative vacuum* (Davidson 2004). The
darksome deep is an ambivalent origin in contrast to a creation under the mechanism of control and mastery that *ex
nihilo* offers. In the beginning is formless, primal chaos, evok-

ing a feminine tehomic language and a refutation of divine omnipotence.

The notion of creation out of nothing is used to emphasize God's ontological being above and beyond all created forms. The alternative account of creation, equally based on exegetical scholarship, is *creatio ex profundis* (Keller 2003, 155ff.). As the name implies, creation arises from the boundless and expanding depths of the chaos-cosmos rather than being zapped into being from nothing. "The beginning" does not mark a single absolute origin but a "beginning-in-process" that is both "unoriginated and endless." According to Wes Howard-Brook (2010, 51) we are dealing with primeval rather than with historical time.

Finally, we come to the creative agent at work: "God's Spirit hovered over the water." According to Christianity there is no conferring of the Spirit until Pentecost (as outlined in Acts 2:1–11). And according to Trinitarian theology the Spirit cannot operate until Father and Son first do their work, so what is the Spirit in Genesis all about? Process theologian Ronald Faber, following the pioneering work of Alfred North Whitehead, suggests that we should understand the story of creation aesthetically rather than causally, with God as the poet of the world erotically luring creation toward self-creativity (Faber 2004, 298).

This God is not the one who orders the universe into a fixed order but rather the luring Spirit who

> arranges creation as an adventure, placing it squarely into openness, accompanying it as open wholeness, and keeping its wholeness open . . . She is instead the Eros that even in her immanence is always transcendent, the Eros in which "order" is actually an abstraction to which no real significance or meaning can be attributed beyond concrete, living, processual intensity and harmony. (Faber 2004, 118, 229)

The Spirit of God being portrayed here defies all the metaphysical boundaries of conventional pneumatology, exhibiting instead several of the key features of the indigenous notion of the Great Spirit (which I describe at length in O'Murchu 2012). In rather esoteric/mystical language Faber describes the Spirit of foundational creativity:

> It is in the ecological embedding and wholeness that the "spiritual" aspect of the spirit resides. This spirit acquires concreteness, however, not through reason, consciousness, or the freedom of decision . . . but through its preconscious spontaneity and unconscious feeling, its inclination towards intensity and its ecstatic causality, its mutual interpenetration of mentality and corporeality, potentiality and actuality, subjectivity and objectivity, subjective inwardness and rigorous self-surpassing—and all of these things within a specific ecological intertwinement.[2] (2004, 287)

Dabar: The Original Creative Energy

John's Gospel opens with a cosmic declaration: "In the beginning was the Word . . . and the Word was God." The Greek word used is *Logos*, which literally means the rational principle, through which everything can be rationally explained. Hellenistic (Greek) influence is clearly discernible. And it is quite probable that the author of John's Gospel was evoking

---

[2] Similar sentiments are expressed by theologian Leonardo Boff in this inspiring quote: "Everything having to do with the force of fascination, attraction, and union, with the solidarity that includes all, with the forgiveness that reconciles, with the communion that bonds and reconnects all, with creative fantasy, innovation, invention, creation, extrapolation, transcendence, ecstasy, newness, complexity, order, beauty, and with the most varied forms of life, has to do with the Spirit" (2013, 34).

the opening sentiments of the book of Genesis whereby God was "pronouncing" creation into being.

According to the book of Genesis, creation happens in the power of the Word. In Hebrew, however, it translates as *Dab(h)ar,* used twenty-four hundred times in the Bible. The Hebrew *Dabar* is used in reference to the "Divine Word," and in an active sense, as a "word-event," or prophetic word. The *Dabar* of the Lord carries with it the ability to accomplish what it is sent to do. It also denotes dynamism, filled with a power that is felt by those who receive it, but that is present independently of such reception. Steven R. Service (2015, 59ff.) provides a detailed analysis of how *Dabar* is used in the Hebrew Scriptures, noting that "Encounter with the Dabar implied impartation of the Spirit" (2015, 74n117). In different books of the Hebrew Scriptures, for example, the Psalms, Proverbs, and Jeremiah, the creation is expressly declared to be the work of Wisdom—for which *Dabar* (the Word-as-action) is frequently used. And the holy *Dabar* is uniquely manifested in the unfolding of creation: The heavens declare the glory of God as the world manifests or reveals the Holy One to our experience.

Memra is the Aramaic for "word," which in the Greek is *Logos.* The concept of the *Memra* is derived from Psalm 33:6: "By the word of the LORD were the heavens made; and all the host of them by the breath of his mouth." As early as the first century CE, interpretations (or paraphrases) of religious passages known as *Targums* began to be written down in Aramaic for Jews who no longer spoke Hebrew. In the *Targums* the Jews used the Aramaic word *Memra,* meaning "word," as a personal manifestation of the presence of God.

The Hebrew *Memra,* the Aramaic *Dabar,* the Greek *Logos* (divine rational principle), and the Greek *Rhema* (utterance or things said) all communicate the *Shekinah* or presence of God as a dynamic, empowering, creative life force, identified primarily with that divine source we call the Holy Spirit of

God (see Service 2015, 46, 74, 99, 178–79, 458, 532). Service (2015, 77, 197) also identifies the unfolding of this creative wisdom with the biblical notion of the kingdom of God, but fails to develop this important insight to the level provided with other contemporary scholars outlined in above.

The central issue at stake here—highlighted throughout in Service's seminal work—is that Greek rationality (captivated in the concept of the *Logos* as rational principle) seriously undermines the creative dynamism inherent in the ancient Hebrew/ Aramaic use of the Word. The Greek epistemological principle of noncontradiction (Service 2015, 35–46) leaves us with a conceptual and linguistic repertoire unable to grasp the creative, dynamic empowerment communicated in the ancient notions of the *Memra/Dabar* of the Hebrew Scriptures. The foundational empowering relationality of the ancient wisdom was subverted amid the Greek desire for logic and rationality. Cold, hard fact took precedence to the mobile amorphous flow of empowering story, captivated in the New Testament in the vision of the kingdom (described in chapter 5 above as the Companionship of Empowerment) and illustrated vividly by Jesus in the parable narratives.

Spirit Encountering Spirit

We now return to the basic premise of the present chapter: *Spirituality essentially means Spirit-encountering-spirit*, suggesting that this encounter provides the nexus through which creativity operates at every level of life, including that of the Godhead itself. First, there is Spirit (with the capital S), the oldest and deepest intuition we humans employ regarding the originating mystery through which everything came into being and is sustained within the open-ended universe.

Next there is spirit (with the small s). This is the same originating imperative operating in every organism, animate and inanimate alike. There is a resonance and congruence between *Spirit* and *spirit* across the entire canopy of God's creation. Essentially, everything is transparent to the lure of in-spirited creativity, and everything is endowed with the capacity to respond appropriately. This invitation-response, however, has to be seen in its primordial context, which is the cosmic web of life, and our human interaction with that web through our God-given propensities as Earthlings. And *Earthlings* is the crucial word we need to emphasize.

As highlighted in chapter 4 above, the Earth is our natural/supernatural God-given home. In the Gospels it is a translation of the original Greek, *oikos,* with its rich, organic meaning explored at length by Michael Crosby (2012). Planet Earth provides the entire context of everything that defines and describes our true human identity. While we remain close to the earth, loving and respecting our status as Earthlings, then we tend to get it right, which means we engage creatively and fruitfully in the engagement of Spirit-with-spirit. When we act out of sync with our earthiness, we set up the forces of alien-ation that damage our own integrity and turn us into the mon-sters who have wreaked so much havoc on the Earth.

Our creativity becomes misplaced and distorted. Dark spirit blocks our access to true spirit—and this has noth-ing to do with Satan or the divine monsters propounded by other religions. The problem is of our own making, arising from our ignorance of the earth and our disconnect from the nourishing womb of our existence. And there is no point waiting for a divine rescuer—Savior or whatever—to come and redeem us, or sort out the mess for us. We have created it, and it is within our power to rectify it. If we fail to do that (a grim prospect, looking increasingly precarious), the wise Earth will, in due course, sort out the problem and find an ingenious way to rid itself of this destructive species that we have chosen to become.

Our Ancient Incarnational Creativity

The prospect of species self-destruction looms over us like a dark cloud. Most frightening of all, it may already be too late to reverse the slippery slope down which we are sliding to ultimate perdition. We certainly cannot reverse our predicament without a massive shift in consciousness, accompanied by a new mode of mutual engagement, what all the religions confusedly call the *call to conversion*. Even if we cannot reverse our plight, we do have options on what kind of collective death we wish to undergo. That, too, depends on a consciousness shift, with spirituality inscribed at its very core.

This spiritual bulwark is an endowment that long predates all the formal religions of recent millennia. We are being invited to reconnect with an ancient wisdom deeply inscribed (by the Spirit) in every fiber of creation, and in the inner being of every human. To paraphrase St. Paul (1 Cor. 2:6–8), it is a wisdom that belongs to the mature, not a wisdom of this age, or of the rulers of this age; if the rulers had understood wisely, they would not have crucified the Lord of glory. Paradoxically, it is not just "the Lord of glory" we have crucified; we have rendered violence to every fiber of creation, both around and within us—all because we lack the integrated wisdom of the Spirit, which is essentially what spirituality is all about.

The monotheistic religions (in particular) got this one badly wrong. By problematizing the living Earth (our primary spirit-filled abode), we have ended up convoluting everything that constitutes our God-given spiritual status. Our often demonic behavior is itself the outcome of our demonization of creation itself, a predicament that can only be resolved by escape to a heavenly dwelling place in the hereafter.

Such a resolution is almost uniquely Christian (and Muslim). The Vedic notion of Nirvana means breaking through the cycle of *samara*, whether in this life or in the hereafter—which in both Hinduism and Buddhism are not dualistically opposed (as in Christianity) but seem to be held in transphysical (material) symbiosis. Nearer to Christianity is Judaism, which for the greater part does not adopt the notion of an afterlife (Raphael 2009; see also http://www.jewfaq.org/olamhaba.htm).

Steven R. Service (2015) illuminates a key element in our confused inheritance. The Hebrew Scripture (OT) frequently alludes to the *ancient life*, which in Greek tends to be translated as *eternal life* (Greek: *aionios zoe*), which literally means "life of the ages," with an ultimate fulfillment in a paradise up ahead, rather than the "heaven on earth" that carried an ancient sense of blessedness (grace) metaphorically highlighted in the Edenic garden of Genesis. Thus Service remarks,

> The purpose of the Scriptures is that these should serve as a roadmap back to the blessing of the ancient life which was intended for all of humankind in God's splendorous garden at the foundation of the world. . . . Pursuit of the ancient life led to love of one's neighbor, the wellbeing of the community, Edenic harmony, embrace of God's daily miraculous help, and a tangible dwelling place in the realm of the Spirit. (2015, 140, 354)

In the New Testament, *eternal life* is translated from the original Greek: *aionios zoe*. The corresponding Hebrew word is rendered *l'olam*, which translates as *world* or *universe*. The ancient root of the word actually means "stretching off into the far distance." For the Jewish scholar Charles A. Rabalai,

> The Hebrew word *olam* means in the far distance. When looking off in the far distance it is difficult to make out any details and what is beyond that horizon cannot be seen. The concept is the *olam*. The word

olam is also used for time for the distant past or the distant future as a time that is difficult to know or perceive. This word is frequently translated as *eternity* or *forever* but in the English language it is misunderstood to mean a continual span of time that never ends. In the Hebrew mind it is simply what is at or beyond the horizon, a very distant time. A common phrase in the Hebrew is *"l'olam va'ed"* and is usually translated as "forever and ever" but in the Hebrew it means *"to the distant horizon and again"* meaning *"a very distant time and even further"* and is used to express the idea of a *"very ancient"* or *"future time."* (www.ancient-hebrew.org/guests_east.html)

For a spirituality of creativity, some key issues arise:

- Time should not be viewed in a linear sequence from past to present and on to the future. Time is lateral rather than linear; the creativity of every now can only be accessed through a symbiosis of past-present-future.
- The foundational wisdom of the past contains wellsprings of origination that are forever being reworked in the dynamic unfolding of evolution's process. However, evolution's primary impetus belongs to the future rather than the past, the "lure of the future" frequently highlighted in the work of theologian John F. Haught (2010; 2015).
- The Christian concept of eternal life projects our search for ultimate meaning to a transcendent future for which earthbound time is a mere preparation, and therefore, of limited value in itself. This understanding seriously undermines the rich, complex tapestry of evolution as well as the creativity of God, animating and sustaining the evolutionary process.

- The Hebrew notion of *olam* (ancient life) captivates the evolutionary dynamic unfolding throughout time and eternity. Although primarily referencing the garden of Eden as the symbol for the fullness of life, authentic time belongs not merely to the ancient past but to the "forever" spectrum of past-present-future.

Many of these insights are congruent with the unfolding wisdom of quantum physics, relocating time in the ever-present and not merely in a nostalgic past or in a falsely utopian future. In biblical language what we need to come to terms with is not *chronos* (chronology) but *kairos*, which denotes opportunity, spontaneity, and creative breakthrough. For the human species it supports additional impetus for reclaiming our ancient evolutionary story, as outlined in the opening chapters of this book. Our patriarchal time capsule (less than ten thousand years old) has shriveled human creativity almost to the point of extinction. This functional horizon, preoccupied with domination and control, is proving disastrous for human well-being at every level. The result is a deep, painful state of alienation, reaching epidemic proportions.

Feeding Our Spiritual Hunger

Millions of people in the contemporary world hunger for spiritual meaning but predominantly through compensatory behaviors. Religiosity itself remains a major delusionary outlet. Others, more widely recognized, include hedonism (addictive pleasure), power seeking, recreational drugs, gambling, and economic consumerism (shopping). We use these escapist behaviors to cover over an inner angst, an alienation that frightens and dislocates our otherwise noble aspirations.

In our compensatory escapist behaviors we are actually worshiping a God of our own making. In some cases it is the divine caricature of formal religion itself. We seek connection with the object of our several false projections, the elusive fulfillment we seek through our addictions. On closer examination these false allurements are not so much anti-God as anti-creation. Our wounded status as Earthlings is at the root of much of our displaced spirituality.

Whether through our patriarchally driven educational systems or through the formal religions themselves, we seek a power outside ourselves—and outside our "world"—that social conditioning has reassured us will enable us to regain a sense of power and control when we encounter the craziness of life. In religious terms we have been indoctrinated into believing that we are fundamentally alienated from God, and only some transcendent escape route can return us to sanity and sanctity. And for fundamentalist Christians, Jesus is the only one who can achieve that.

As indicated elsewhere in this book, the unquestioned assumption that salvation can only be guaranteed in a world beyond lies at the root of all our alienations. It deceives us into thinking that escape from this vale of tears is the only authentic option, or alternatively, that we can overcome our angst with the growing proliferation of hedonistic distractions. In our confused, alienated state we miss the truth staring us in the face: we are Earthlings, and our convivial relationship with the living Earth itself is how we become what evolution makes possible for us.

The Earth-organicity that alone can satisfy our deepest longings and desires is where we first encounter the creative energy of the Great Spirit. This is where all authentic spirituality begins, and it unfolds from there in the invitation to befriend the Great Spirit in the evolutionary renewal of cosmic and planetary life. For Christians, Jesus assuredly is an inspiring model as a Spirit-filled person, pointing us always to that more foundational source of life and meaning. When we make

Jesus—or the Buddha or Muhammad—an end in themselves, then the alienation begins to set in.

It is spirituality that keeps creativity alive in Scripture, theology, and in all the wisdom that connects us meaningfully with our grounding in God's creation. All the religions attempt this connectedness within specific cultural and time-bound contexts. All the major religions we know today evolved under the shadow of postagricultural patriarchy; consequently all are tainted—to varying degrees—by patriarchy's compulsive drive toward domination and control. Spirituality, on the other hand, delivers the urgings of the Spirit for the archetypal, the primordial, the new, and that which awakens and sustains creativity at every level.[3]

---

[3] Of course spirituality can become deviant and destructive as well. The total dismissal of religion in favor of spirituality requires a quality of discernment that is often lacking on both sides of the divide. Carrette and King (2005) highlight how contemporary market forces have invaded the spiritual awakening of our time and distorted several of its key elements. Several "New Age" charlatans apply the label of spirituality to a range of esoteric practices that can certainly awaken creative potential but in the hands of the uninitiated can wreak havoc on health and well-being.

10

The Creativity of Divine Insistence

Revelation is an in-coming, a breaking-in upon the world that takes the world by surprise. That is not "super-natural" but an amplitude of the way the world works. To live in history is to be structurally subject to surprise, to unforeseeability, to the future.

—John D. Caputo

Creativity is attended by the gentle art of a patient hand, pressing this ruthless chaotic flood into events with meaning and beauty. . . . This is the power of the Spirit that is in God, and at work in each of us in the world.

—Bernard Meland

Several theologians, ancient and modern, allude to a quality of creativity uniquely embodied in our very notion of God, manifested in God's love and care for our world. Some go much further, asserting that this foundational creativity is innate to creation itself, as indicated in the words of the opening quote above: "the way the world works." My first acquaintance with this notion came through two works of the American theologian Gordon D. Kaufman (2004; 2006), his first volume focusing on God's creativity, and the second one exploring how Jesus embodies that same creativity in a more grounded way.

Kaufman proposes that we conceive of God as a process of creative activity rather than as a personal supernatural being, describing the trajectories of creativity as interwoven through the long history of the universe and also through the evolutionary history of our planet. In human beings, that creative process combined biological and historical-cultural dimensions into a symbolic, spiritual, moral, and yet thoroughly bodily species, for which the historical Jesus serves as an exemplary model.

We are deeply entangled in our amazingly fecund ecological context, and yet we are also capable of creatively transcending our environment through understanding and influencing it. Not all creative trajectories are conducive to human flourishing, but serendipitous elements of creativity make our existence possible and support our cultural and personal aspirations. It is those aspects that we most strongly identify with the word "God." We are the creative fruit of serendipitous creativity itself.

Several of Kaufman's "trajectories" are further illuminated in the present work. In this concluding chapter I want to highlight some of the key dimensions I have noted, adopting seminal and controversial insights from the radical theologian John Caputo (2013). Using select quotations from Caputo's work, I briefly outline some promising horizons that merit further discerning wisdom amid the evolutionary flux of the twenty-first century. This ongoing discernment is marked by a significant departure from the metaphysical certainties of the past to the mystical exploration that characterizes our time with a fresh acuity.

1. *"God is a spirit who calls, a spirit that can happen anywhere and haunts everything insistently. . . . As to the big picture, the large course the Spirit traverses, the large circle it*

always cuts, there is no maybe about it; it must be what it must be" (Caputo 2013, 131).

My take on creativity as a foundational feature of God, along with all that God has created and sustains, is foundationally inspired by the notion of the Great Spirit, as upheld by indigenous peoples ancient and modern. Faith in the Great Spirit begins with grace, the graciousness of proclivity, characterized by a creative energy that brings everything into being and sustains all throughout creation's evolutionary unfolding. It recaptures afresh the divine reassurance of Genesis 1: "God saw that it was good." That is the starting point articulated to one degree or another by every major religion, yet rarely if ever honored by the religions, particularly as they evolve into patriarchal institutionalization. As the British Scripture scholar Tom Wright repeatedly reminds us, God's revelation (read: creativity) in the Judeo-Christian context is predominantly about creation rather than salvation.

As indicated in chapter 9 above, the Spirit of God plays a dynamic role in the story of creation (Genesis 1), the implications of which have been poorly acknowledged in Christian pneumatology. Relegating the Holy Spirit to third place in the Trinitarian triad, highlighting the conferring of the Holy Spirit at Pentecost, and attributing a special endowment of the Holy Spirit at Baptism for personal alignment with God—all distract from and undermine the foundational role of the Spirit as outlined in the opening chapter of Genesis.

When we allow the wisdom of the Great Spirit in the indigenous traditions to inform our understanding of the Holy Spirit, we open up theological and scriptural possibilities that are quite revolutionary. At the fore is the topic explored in the present book. Throughout creation (including humans) we witness an insinuated creative imperative that brings everything into being and sustains all that exists and unfolds. It involves a great deal more than the traditional role attributed to the foundational creator, usually described as God the Father. This is a transpersonal energizer of profound and inexhaustible potential (in Caputo's words, "haunting everything insistently"), and with a cosmic reach transcending time and space (without beginning or end). Yet, paradoxically, the most enduring manifestation of this Spirit at work is in the material creation itself, the complex evolving universe, and the organic earthiness of our home planet.

2. *"There is grace, grace happens, but it is the grace of the world. . . . My entire idea is to reclaim religion as an event of this world, to reclaim religion for the world, and the world for religion"* (Caputo 2013, 346–47).

The religions have not honored that initial divine imperative: all is grace! Even the paradoxical elements of creation-cum-destruction need to be viewed within this foundational horizon of meaning. Not until our species takes this imperative as our central focus—in ecology, politics, economics, education, social policy, health care—do we stand any realistic hope of engaging our life-call with truth and integrity. Our current attempts at creativity, fueled by consumption, manipulation, competition, violence, and religious bigotry, are not merely unsustainable but are certain to reap worse and worse rewards for *Homo sapiens* within a matter of decades.

Creative grace is not about escape from this vale of tears to a utopian paradise hereafter. That is just one of our several cruel delusions. As coworkers for and with the Great Spirit, our spiritual integrity is deeply embedded in the living Earth itself. There is no heavenly world beyond, or anywhere else to which we can escape. We come to terms with this sacred space, or from there on we condemn ourselves to mass alienation.

As indicated earlier, this marks a significant theological shift, from the Christian focus on salvation to the enlarged challenge of encountering the living God in creation itself. It posits creation as God's original and most enduring revelation of divine elegance and creativity. It requires a reframing of every religious system that humans have evolved in historical time. It seeks to transcend the anthropocentric portrayal of Holy Mystery in favor of a Spirit-inebriated creation, for which the notion of the Great Spirit seems to be the most authentic and empowering catalyst. It could also be described as a new mysticism for our age, albeit one with deep ancient roots.

3. "*I am trying to stage a coup that steals the word 'theology' out from under the nose of the palace theologians and use these stolen goods to haunt the house of the pious. . . . My idea is to break the crust of piety, to call out the princes of the church and shame them into doing honest work, to break the idols of religious authorities wherever they rear their head, whether under the cover of a book or an institution*" (Caputo 2013, 25, 26).

The theologians more than anybody else have dislodged the Great Spirit. Preoccupied with the metaphysics of the "palace," they have bequeathed to us a theodicy of power and domination that is proving to be highly destructive of people and planet alike. Inadvertently they have reinforced the conquering power of rationality, thus reinforcing the emergence of religious institutions that cannot tolerate the energizing creativity of the living Earth itself. Thus the theologians cling to the dualistic splitting of secular vs. sacred, body vs. soul, matter vs. spirit.

In Caputo's timely words, we need to break the idolatry of religious authorities and return spirituality to where it primarily belongs, namely to the creative fertility of the earth itself, infused by the ever pregnant wisdom of the Great Spirit. This is where both piety and theology begin, with the *sensus fidelium* as the primary reservoir of revealed truth. This is the "honest work" to which Caputo alludes: the willingness to dialogue with those organic sources of divine revelation that predate and underpin both metaphysics and doctrinal assertions.

It brings the religious authorities on the one hand and the theologians on the other out from the secluded imperial space of the palace (read: institution) to engage not merely the wider human population but the entire web of life in its cosmic and planetary grandeur. Few theologians alive today were trained in this enlarged horizon of meaning. For the future it is the escapable realm of the new theological creativity.

4. *"The new cosmology is taking our breath away with speculative leaps that have opened up a cosmological 'perhaps' that has stolen philosophy's thunder (which is wonder). It has rendered obsolete the old pre-Copernican mythopoetics to which theology has too long been wedded and shaken our most basic presuppositions about 'human' and 'life' and 'matter,' exposing them to a 'perhaps' we never imagined"* (Caputo 2013, 22). *"God is an insistence whose existence can only be found in matter, space, and time. Where else could God be God?"* (Caputo 2013, 163).

Throughout the present work I present the new cosmology and quantum physics as alternative articulations of a way of seeing and understanding our world, with substantive readjustments for every sphere of human learning. Both bodies of wisdom invite us to outgrow the imperial, controlling anthropocentrism that has kept humans as a dominant and superior species for far too long. Both sciences have also demolished our hierarchical linear worldviews in favor of a relational matrix, where all beings are invited into unprecedented levels of interdependence and interconnectedness.

While every religion is drawn to a Trinitarian understanding of God, couched in either mystical or metaphysical concepts, the human species has carried a creative hunch over several millennia that God is a great deal more than a metaphysical construct of three-in-one. It is our ancient (some might say primitive) creative intuition of life's primordial relationality that in time was translated into religious doctrines. The doctrines did not come first and then the relational intuitions; quite the contrary, it was our ancient ancestors grounded in the relational web of life who first came to know God as the foundational infrastructure of all relationality (and proceeded to name it doctrinally as Trinity).

Just as we can no longer discern the meaning of the universe through a literal rational reading of reality, neither can we apprehend the deeper meaning of the mystery within which we exist and flourish. All truth is mystical, metaphorical, and symbolic. All creation is a parable, every bit as complex and profound as the parable stories of Jesus in the Gospels. Creativity abounds in what Caputo calls *mythopoetics*, an articulation of the embracing mystery requiring a quality of discernment that goes beyond every formal religion and beyond all sacred texts.

And this is what leads to the irrational fears that hold modern cultures and religions in their tenacious grip: if we don't know who is in charge, who is ultimately responsible for safeguarding truth, then we could all be consumed by terrorists! But that's not the case if we learn to love our enemies and mobilize our creative resources for nonviolent empowerment. It is hard to imagine our patriarchal rulers moving in that direction, but I suspect time will prove to us that it is the only viable option. Like it or not, evolution won't wait for patriarchal plans but will move on without us, and it is up to those of us in the ready to seize the moment and befriend the evolving expansive horizons.

5. *"The 'kingdom of God' in the New Testament is an exceptionally ironic 'kingdom,' a most anarchic monarchy, upside-down and turning on topsy-turvy reversals. It is made up of a striking assembly of very unroyal rogues, of very earthy bodies woven from the elements. And of bodies unraveling under the press of elemental breakdown"* (Caputo 2013, 252).

While I pride myself in being a multifaith believer, with a passionate desire for multifaith dialogue and almost three decades outgrowing religion in favor of a more mystical trans-religious consciousness, I have to concede that I find something insatiably satisfying in the vision of Jesus. That something is what the Gospels describe as the kingdom of God, my understanding of which is outlined in chapter 6 above.

Within that unique vision I certainly deserve to be called an "unroyal rogue," because I subscribe to very little of creed-based Christianity. My fundamental disagreement is with the very language the Gospels adopt: the Greek *Basileia tou theou* translates into the *Kingdom of God*, with the many imperial echoes of those words. I cannot accept anymore that those are the actual words Jesus used, so I opt instead for the Aramaic-based Companionship of Empowerment. That vision certainly turns upside-down the power mongering so endemic to all the Christian churches.

Fidelity to this new Companionship requires an enormous amount of creativity, as illustrated in the parable and miracle narratives of the New Testament. Most empowering of all are the connections that begin to emerge. That same capacity for deep relating that we encountered in the new cosmology and in quantum physics we now see staring us in the face from the matrix of this new Companionship. At every level of life the primary challenge is to get our relationships right, through empowering mutuality within the cosmic, planetary, and human webs of life.

6. *"Hospitality cuts deeply into the fabric of the biblical name of God, where the invisible face of God is inscribed on the face of the stranger, as if God were looking for shelter"* (Caputo 2013, 39).

The imperial kingdom of God, like the kingdom of Caesar, among so many others, engendered creativity through the philosophy of divide-and-conquer, based on a spirituality of hostility, offering no "shelter." The new Companionship is postulated unambiguously on a spirituality of hospitality, inclusivity, and nonviolence. Not merely are all outsiders invited in, but the outsider holds the place of honor.

In the commensality of the Gospels, not merely are the prostitutes, tax collectors, and sinners included. They are actually the ones who hold the primary right to be at table with Jesus, and they were not asked to repent and thus make themselves worthy to be included. Reformation is no longer the task at hand; transformation is. The last are first, and the first are banished. Even the holy temple has been ransacked!

And let's continue to be vigilant around reductionism. We have been indoctrinated in keeping things small and manageable; it feeds into our patriarchal addiction of domination and control. Hospitality is not just about humans and our ways of engaging each other. The abundant proclivity of the universe and planet Earth is the foundational hospitality, acknowledging the highly destructive forces that are integral to such abundance. All is gift, and we need to come to terms with that prodigious truth; otherwise we are setting ourselves on a sure road to perdition.

Such hospitality brings us full circle. The hospitable Earth is itself a place of welcoming shelter, home to the Great Spirit, whose creative energy exudes through every being. And everybody is needed—saint and sinner alike—to bring about the inspirited/inspired reign of God, the new heaven amid the renewed earth. Could any endeavor be more worthy of creative creatures, coworking with our creative God?

Afterthought

Where Are We Going with Original Sin?

In the opening chapter I referenced the compendium on original sin by Cavanaugh and Smith (2017), which, among other things, highlights the original and fundamental goodness of God's creation, as outlined in Genesis 1. Recall the repeated mantra: *God saw that it was good.* Why then do all the religions set out to rectify a fundamental wrong, instead of celebrating a fundamental good? Suppose Christianity adopted the primordial goodness as its starting point, which is neither ignoring nor denying sin and evil. Then we would need a very different politics, economics, educational systems, social policies, and so on. Also, the chances are that we would have a very different world, more congruent with the relational empowerment that belongs to the archetypal garden of Eden.

For almost ten thousand years religion has focused primarily not on grace but on the notions of sin and evil. And what have we achieved from that strategy? Have we made the world a better place? Have we brought happiness and fulfillment to humans? Have we benefited the Earth and all its creatures? My hunch is that the primary focus on sin and evil has actually exacerbated the problems we evidence each day. This outlook also betrays that fundamental creativity at the heart of our being. Focusing on the dark side of life has done little to illuminate the mystery within which we all live and have our being. The more we try to rid the world of evil, the more we seem to create new demons.

Wisely, therefore, the Orthodox Christian communities give relatively little attention to original sin and the fundamental flaw. True to the spirit of St. Paul, they highlight grace and not sin. They describe the human journey into wholeness as one of *deification*. In Orthodox thought, Adam and Eve are understood to be blessed with a special calling: to become one with God through a gradual process of growth into God's own holiness, hence the notion of deification. Accordingly, original sin is not so much a state of guilt inherited from Adam but an unnatural condition of human life that ends in death (more in the classic exposition of Romanides 2002).

The Orthodox tradition has also developed the complementary notion of *theosis*, suggesting that human beings can have real union with God, and so become like God to such a degree that we participate in the divine nature. Theosis and deification are often used interchangeably (see Keating 2007). Such spirituality invites the devotee to embrace and follow an inner lure of the Spirit, prioritizing the foundational goodness of all in God's creation. This sounds remarkably similar to the belief in the Great Spirit adopted by indigenous / First Nations peoples throughout the contemporary world, as outlined in a previous work (O'Murchu 2012).

But how can we follow this lure—the foundational creative instinct—when we have been otherwise indoctrinated for so long? Can we transcend our moralistic conditioning and choose another route to wholeness and well-being? From religion to politics, across the entire spectrum of learning and action, we are told that it all begins with a problem that must be contained and tolerated. Why not begin with the vast horizons of creative possibility, with the abundance of creation, and not merely the postulated scarcity of resources? Creation in its cosmic range and planetary resourcefulness is full of promise and possibility; it feels like *Homo sapiens* is no longer capable of engaging these vast potentials. In our reductionistic mechanical engagement with creation, even our own inner being has shrunk and shriveled.

I began this concluding reflection with the question, where are we going with original sin? *My sense is that we are going nowhere.* We seem to be stuck in a dead end, with no obvious way out. One wonders why the theologians still go on trying to make sense of a doctrine that has wreaked so much havoc and paralyzed so much human creativity. At the other end of the spectrum are the thousands (perhaps millions) who have dumped the baby with the bathwater, who neither care nor resonate with religious moralism. The churches and religions are quick to condemn them as reckless and immoral. But are they? Perhaps they are the prophets of an alternative future, recapitulating an ancient graced wisdom, a primordial creativity, arising like an evolutionary imperative from the cosmic creation itself.

Might this be our greatest hope? What we humans cannot achieve for ourselves, perhaps creation can bring about in a liberating breakthrough. I suspect it will not be the first time in evolutionary history in which creation rescued humans from their wayward ways. Nor will it be the first time—following the bold suggestion of sociologist Pitrim Sorokin—in which the internal barbarians became the saviors of civilization!

Bibliography

Aalen, Sverre. 1962. "'Reign' and 'House' in the Kingdom of God in the Gospels." *New Testament Studies* 8, 215–40.

Abram, David. 1996. *The Spell of the Sensuous*. New York: Vintage Books.

———. 2010. *Becoming Animal: An Earthly Cosmology*. New York: Vintage Books.

Armstrong, Karen. 1996. *In the Beginning*. London: Vintage.

Assmann, Jon. 2010. *The Price of Monotheism*. Stanford, CA: Stanford University Press.

Barker, Graeme. 2009. *The Agricultural Revolution in Prehistory*. Oxford: Oxford University Press.

Bauckham, Richard. 2002. *Gospel Women*. Grand Rapids: Eerdmans.

Becker, Udo. 1994. *The Continuum Encyclopedia of Symbols*. New York: Continuum.

Beltran, Benigno. 2012. *Faith and Struggle on Smokey Mountain*. Maryknoll, NY: Orbis.

Bermejo-Rubio, Fernando. 2014. "Jesus and the Anti-Roman Resistance: A Reassessment of the Argument," *Journal of the Study of the Historical Jesus* 12, 1–105.

Boff, Leonardo. 2013. *Christianity in a Nutshell*. Maryknoll, NY: Orbis.

————. 2015. *Come, Holy Spirit*. Maryknoll, NY: Orbis.

Borg, Marcus, & John D. Crossan. 2006. *The Last Week*. San Francisco: HarperSanFrancisco.

Boulton, David. 2008. *Who on Earth Was Jesus?* Winchester (UK): O Books.

Campbell, Charlie. 2013. *Scapegoat: A History of Blaming Other People*. New York: Overlook Press.

Caputo, John D. 2013. *The Insistence of God: A Theology of Perhaps*. Bloomington: Indiana University Press.

Carrette, Jeremy, & Richard King. 2005. *Selling Spirituality*. New York: Routledge.

Cavanaugh, William T., & James K. A. Smith. 2017. *Evolution and the Fall*. Grand Rapids: Eerdmans.

Chabal, Patrick. 2012. *The End of Conceit: Western Rationality after Postcolonialism*. New York: Zed Books.

Chopra, Deepak, & Menas Kafatos. 2017. *You Are the Universe*. London: Rider Books.

Christ, Carol, & Judith Plaskow. 2016. *Goddesses and God in the World*. Minneapolis: Fortress Press.

Christian, David. 2004. *Maps of Time: An Introduction to Big History*. Berkeley: University of California Press.

Christie, Douglas E. 2013. *The Blue Sapphire of the Mind: Notes for a Contemplative Ecology*. New York: Oxford University Press.

Church, Dawson. 2014. *The Genie in Your Genes*. Fulton, CA: Energy Psychology Press.

Clottes, Jean, & David Lewis-Williams. 1998. *The Shamans of Prehistory*. New York: Abrams Books.

Collins, Christopher. 2013. *Paleopoetics: The Evolution of the Preliterate Imagination*. New York: Columbia University Press.

Conway Morris, Simon. 2003. *Life's Solution*. Cambridge: Cambridge University Press.

Cook, Jill. 2013. *Ice Age Art: The Arrival of the Modern Mind*. London: British Museum Press.

Cooper, Kate. 2013. *Band of Angels: The Forgotten World of Early Christian Women*. London: Atlantic Books.

Crosby, Michael H. 2012. *Repair My House!* Maryknoll, NY: Orbis.

Crossan, John Dominic. 1991. *The Historical Jesus*. San Francisco: HarperSanFrancisco.

———. 1997. "Jesus and the Kingdom." In *Jesus at 2000*, ed. Marcus Borg, 21–53. Boulder, CO: Westview Press.

———. 1998. *The Birth of Christianity*. San Francisco: HarperSanFrancisco.

———. 2010. *The Greatest Prayer*. New York: HarperCollins.

Davidson, John. 2004. *The Secret of the Creative Vacuum: Man and the Energy Dance*. New York: Random House.

Davies, Paul. 1993. *The Mind of God: Science and the Search for Ultimate Meaning*. New York: Penguin.

Deacon, Terence. 1997. *The Symbolic Species*. New York: Allen Lane/Penguin.

Delio, Ilia, ed. 2014. *From Teilhard to Omega*. Maryknoll, NY: Orbis.

———. 2015. *Making All Things New*. Maryknoll, NY: Orbis.

Dill, Karen E. 2009. *How Fantasy Becomes Reality*. New York: Oxford University Press.

Drucker, Peter. 1995. *The Age of Discontinuity*. New York: Routledge.

Eisenstein, Charles. 2011. *Sacred Economics*. Berkeley, CA: Evolver Editions.

Eliade, Mircea. 1961. *The Sacred and the Profane*. New York: Harper & Row.

———. 1963. *Myth and Reality*. New York: Harper & Row.

Ellingson, Ter. 2001. *The Myth of the Noble Savage*. Berkeley: University of California Press.

Faber, Roland. 2004. *God as Poet of the World*. Louisville, KY: Westminster John Knox Press.

Fiensy, David A. 2014. *Christian Origins and the Ancient Economy*. Eugene, OR: Cascade Books.

Flannery, Kent, & Joyce Marcus. 2012. *The Creation of Inequality*. Cambridge, MA: Harvard University Press.

Fox, Everett. 1983. *The Five Books of Moses*. New York: Schocken.

Fox, Matthew. 1984. *Original Blessing*. Santa Fe, NM: Bear & Co.

Girard, Rene. 1986. *The Scapegoat*. Baltimore, MD: Johns Hopkins University Press.

Gowlett, John A. 1984. *Ascent to Civilization*. New York: McGraw-Hill.

————. 2011. "The Vital Sense of Proportion." *Paleoanthropology*: 174–87.

Greco, Thomas. 2009. *The End of Money*. Edinburgh: Floris Books.

Harari, Yuval Noah. 2015. *Sapiens: A Brief History of Humankind*. New York: HarperCollins.

Haughey, John C. 2015. *A Biography of the Spirit*. Maryknoll, NY: Orbis.

Haught, John F. 2010. *Making Sense of Evolution*. Louisville, KY: Westminster John Knox Press.

————. 2015. *Resting on the Future*. New York: Bloomsbury.

Hawken, Paul. 2007. *Blessed Unrest*. New York: Viking.

Henshilwood, Christopher S., et al. 2011. "A 100,000-Year-Old Ochre-Processing Workshop at Blombos Cave, South Africa." *Science* 334, 219–22.

Herzog, William. 1994. *Parables as Subversive Speech*. Louisville, KY: Westminster/John Knox Press.

Howard-Brook, Wes. 2010. *"Come Out, My People!" God's Call out of Empire in the Bible and Beyond.* Maryknoll, NY: Orbis.

———. 2016. *Empire Baptized: How the Church Embraced What Jesus Rejected.* Maryknoll, NY: Orbis.

Hull, R. F., and J. Jacobi, eds. 1978. *C. G. Jung: Psychological Reflections.* Princeton, NJ: Princeton University Press.

Jeans, James. 1930. *The Mysterious Universe.* Cambridge: Cambridge University Press.

Johnson, Elizabeth. 2015. *Ask the Beasts: Darwin and the God of Love.* New York: Bloomsbury Continuum.

Johnson, Kurt, and David R. Ord. 2012. *The Coming Interspiritual Age.* Vancouver: Namaste.

Kafatos, Menas. 2013. *The Conscious Universe.* New York: Springer.

Kaufman, Gordon D. 2004. *In the Beginning . . . Creativity.* Minneapolis: Fortress Press.

———. 2006. *Jesus and Creativity.* Minneapolis: Fortress Press.

Keating, Daniel. 2007. *Deification and Grace.* Notre Dame, IN: Sapientia Press.

Keller, Catherine. 2003. *Face of the Deep: A Theology of Becoming.* New York: Routledge.

Kim, Grace Ji-Sun. 2011. *The Holy Spirit, Chi, and the Other.* New York: Palgrave Macmillan.

Kloppenborg, John S. 1982. "Isis and Sophia in the Book of Wisdom," *Harvard Theological Review* 75: 57–84.

Knitter, Paul F. 1985. *No Other Name? A Critical Survey of Christian Attitudes toward the World Religions.* Maryknoll, NY: Orbis.

Kolbert, Elizabeth. 2014. *The Sixth Extinction: An Unnatural History.* New York: Henry Holt & Co.

Kramer, Ross, & Mary Rose d'Angelo. 1999. *Women and Christian Origins.* Oxford: Oxford University Press.

Kraybill, Donald B. 1990. *The Upside Down Kingdom*. Scotdale, PA: Herald Press.

Leakey, Richard, & Roger Lewin. 1996. *The Sixth Extinction*. New York: Anchor Books.

Lee, Jung Young. 1979. *The Theology of Change*. Maryknoll, NY: Orbis.

Lenzi, Alan. 2006. "Proverbs 8:22–31: Three Perspectives on Its Composition." *Journal of Biblical Literature* 125: 687–714.

Lévi-Strauss, Claude. 1978. *Myth and Meaning*. London: Routledge & Kegan Paul.

Lewis-Williams, David. 2002. *The Mind in the Cave*. London: Thames & Hudson.

Liebert, Elizabeth. 2015. *The Soul of Discernment*. Louisville, KY: Westminster John Knox Press.

Lietaer, Bernard. 2001. *The Future of Money*. London: Century Books.

Lovelock, James. 1979. *Gaia: A New Look at Life on Earth*. New York: Oxford University Press.

————. 1988. *The Ages of Gaia*. New York: Oxford University Press.

Maehle, Gregor. 2012. *Pranayama: The Breath of Yoga*. New Delhi: Kaivalya Publications.

Malone, Mary T. 2014. *The Elephant in the Church*. Dublin: Columba Press.

Manning, Richard. 2004. *Against the Grain: How Agriculture Has Hijacked Civilization*. Berkeley, CA: North Point Press.

————. 2014. *Go Wild: Free Your Body and Mind from the Afflictions of Civilization*. Boston: Little, Brown & Co.

Marean, C. W., et al. 2007. "Early Human Use of Marine Resources and Pigment in South Africa during the Middle Pleistocene." *Nature* 449: 905–8.

McCaul, T. 2007. *Yoga as Medicine*. New York: Bantam Books.

McFague, Sallie. 2000. *Life Abundant*. Minneapolis: Fortress Press.

McFarland, Ian. 2010. *In Adam's Fall: A Meditation on the Christian Doctrine of Original Sin*. New York: Wiley-Blackwell.

McIntosh, Christopher. 2004. *Gardens of the Gods: Myth, Magic, and Meaning*. London: I. B. Taurus.

Meier, John P. 2009. *A Marginal Jew*. Vol. 4. New Haven, CT: Yale University Press.

Moberg, Mark. 2013. *Engaging Anthropological Theory*. New York: Routledge.

Nuismer, Scott. 2017. *Introduction to Co-evolutionary Theory*. New York: W. F. Freeman.

Oakley, Kenneth P. 1949. *Man the Tool-Maker*. London: British Museum.

O'Murchu, Diarmuid. 2002. *Evolutionary Faith*. Maryknoll, NY: Orbis.

———. 2007. *The Transformation of Desire: How Desire Became Corrupted—And How We Can Reclaim It*. Maryknoll, NY: Orbis.

———. 2008. *Ancestral Grace*. Maryknoll, NY: Orbis.

———. 2010. *Adult Faith*. Maryknoll, NY: Orbis.

———. 2011. *Christianity's Dangerous Memory*. New York: Crossroad.

———. 2012. *In the Beginning Was the Spirit*. Maryknoll, NY: Orbis.

———. 2014a. *On Being a Postcolonial Christian*. North Charleston, SC: CreateSpace.

———. 2014b. *The Meaning and Practice of Faith*. Maryknoll, NY: Orbis.

———. 2015. *Inclusivity: A Gospel Mandate*. Maryknoll, NY: Orbis.

———. 2017. *Incarnation: A New Evolutionary Threshold*. Maryknoll, NY: Orbis.

Osiek, Carolyn, & Margaret MacDonald. 2006. *A Woman's Place*. Minneapolis: Fortress Press.

Parsons, Keith M. 2004. *The Great Dinosaur Controversy*. Santa Barbara, CA: ABC-CLIO.

Patterson, Stephen J. 2014. *The Lost Way*. New York: HarperOne.

Phipps, Carter. 2012. *Evolutionaries*. New York: Harper.

Plumwood, Val. 2002. *Environmental Culture: The Ecological Crisis of Reason*. New York: Routledge.

Pringle, Heather. 2013. "The Origins of Creativity." *Scientific American* 308: 37–43.

Raphael, Simcha Paull. 2009. *Jewish Views of the Afterlife*. Lanham, MD: Rowman & Littlefield.

Reid-Bowen, Paul. 2007. *Goddess as Nature: Towards a Philosophical Thealogy*. Burlington, VT: Ashgate.

Renfrew, Colin. 2009. *The Sapient Mind: Archaeology Meets Neuroscience*. New York: Oxford University Press.

Rifkin, Jeremy. 2009. *The Empathic Civilization*. New York: J. P. Tarcher.

Romanides, John S. 2002. *The Ancestral Sin*. Brookline, MA: Zephyr Publishing.

Rose, Michael R., & Todd H. Oakley. 2007. "The New Biology: Beyond the Modern Synthesis." *Biology Direct* 2: 2–30.

Rowley, Matthew. 2014. "What Causes Religious Violence?" *Journal of Religion and Violence* 3: 361–402.

Sapp, J. 2003. *The Evolution of Biology*. New York: Oxford University Press.

Schafer, Lothar. 2013. *Infinite Potential*. New York: Random House.

Schedtler, Justin J. 2017. "Mother of Gods, Mother of Harlots." *Novum Testamentum* 59: 52–70.

Schüssler Fiorenza, Elisabeth. 1983. *In Memory of Her*. London: SCM Press.

Schwager, Raymund. 2000. *Must There Be Scapegoats?* New York: Herder & Herder.

Schweitzer, Don. 2010. *Contemporary Christologies.* Minneapolis: Fortress Press.

Segal, Robert A. 2004. *Myth: A Very Short Introduction.* Oxford: Oxford University Press.

Service, Steven R. 2015. *The Lost and Forgotten Gospel of the Kingdom.* n.p.: n.p. (self-published).

Sheehan, Thomas. 1986. *The First Coming: How the Kingdom of God Became Christianity.* New York: Random House.

Snodgrass, John. 2011. *Genesis and the Rise of Civilization.* North Charleston, SC: CreateSpace.

Spina, Frank Anthony. 2006. *The Faith of the Outsider: Exclusion and Inclusion in the Biblical Story.* Grand Rapids: Eerdmans.

Spong, John Shelby. 1998. *Why Christianity Must Change or Die.* New York: HarperOne.

———. 2007. *Jesus for the Non-Religious.* San Francisco: HarperCollins.

———. 2016. *Biblical Literalism: A Gentile Heresy.* New York: HarperCollins.

Stevens, Anthony. 1993. *The Two-Million-Year-Old Self:* College Station: Texas A&M University Press.

Stewart, John. 2000. *Evolution's Arrow.* Canberra: Chapman Press.

Stout, Dietrich. 2016. "Tales of a Stone Age Neuroscientist." *Scientific American* 314: 19–27.

Stringer, Chris. 2012. *The Origin of Our Species.* London: Allen Lane.

Taylor, Steve. 2005. *The Fall.* Winchester (UK): O Books.

Thompson, J. N. 1994. *The Coevolutionary Process.* Chicago: University of Chicago Press.

Thorsrud, Harald. 2015. "Aristotle's Dichotomous Anthropology: What Is Most Human in the *Nicomachean Ethics?" Apeiron* 48: 346–67.

van Eck, Ernest. 2016. *The Parables of Jesus the Galilean.* Eugene, OR: Wipf & Stock.

Wiley, Tatha. 2002. *Original Sin: Origins, Developments, Contemporary Meanings.* New York: Paulist Press.

Williams, Patricia. 2001. *Doing without Adam and Eve.* Minneapolis: Fortress Press.

Williamson, Marianne. 1992. *A Return to Love.* New York: HarperCollins.

Wilson Schaef, Anne. 1988. *When Society Becomes an Addict.* New York: HarperOne.

Wink, Walter. 1992. *The Powers That Be.* Minneapolis: Fortress Press.

Index

ANOMIE
Anthropology
Gaia Theory ✓ } LAND

1 Clan totum — Animals
Kinship gathering — noble
2 Tribe — more formal development
3 Chiefdoms hierarched
4 Covenant — promised land.
Responsible evolving group

Hinduism
Brahman the creator
Vishnu the preserver
Shiva the destroyer / regenerator } divine interaction

Buddhism
Nirvana — liberation